PROFESSIONAL PLANS FOR OUTDOOR PROJECTS

Augustus Suglia, A.I.A.

ARCO PUBLISHING, INC.
NEW YORK

Published by Arco Publishing, Inc.
215 Park Avenue South, New York, N.Y. 10003

Project Editor, Allen D. Bragdon

Designer, John B. Miller

This book was produced and edited by Allen D. Bragdon Pub-
lishers, Inc. from designs created and drawn by Augustus Suglia
A.I.A. for a column entitled "Your Home Plans" owned and syn-
dicated by KING FEATURES 235 East 45th Street, New York 10017.

ISBN 0 668 0 5787 4   (hardcover)
ISBN 0 668 0 5790 4   (papercover)

© 1983 King Features Syndicate, Inc.

Table of Contents

Editor's Preface

The plans we have collected for this book are professional building drawings for medium to larger structures within the reach of the non-professional carpenter. They were designed by Augustus Suglia A.I.A., a registered practicing architect with 26 years of experience in residential building. In addition to being a member of the American Institute of Architects and licensed by both the states of New York and New Jersey, his qualifications are certified by the National Council of Architectural Registration Boards.

Some of these plans show how to construct fairly simple, weekend projects for the backyard. Others, like the garages in the back of the book, take some substantial investments in time and materials costs. But most of those are designed so they can be adapted and finished

as residences, for summer vacations or year round. Even keeping the garage space, most of the plans have living accomodations built into them that could become an income-producing rental apartment. The house pictured on this page was built by a fellow in Virginia taking off from plan Number 19 in this book. Although these plans are drawn by a professional, details of critical spots are shown so a non-professional can tackle the project successfully if he can handle tools and knows how to read a plan.

We think you will find that these structures of Augustus Suglia's are unusually practical. As the father of seven children in various age brackets, he designs plenty of storage in the handiest places and with dimensions that fit the items people would be likely to store there as an everyday, practical matter. His residential designs—from a playhouse to a full home—put every square foot to good use yet they avoid bottlenecks because he seems to have thought through the most likely traffic circulation patterns between adjacent spaces. We expect, too, that you may be pleasantly surprised at the way the construction cost per square foot works out. These designs minimize materials waste without sacrificing their structural integrity, practicality or good looks.

We hope that you and your family will have a good time living in and around some of these projects and that you will enjoy putting them together.

The Editor

Suglia Architect

235 East 45th Street New York, N.Y., 10017

Dear Home Owner:

Thank you for your interest in these project plans.

These plans are designed so that they can be easily adapted to existing conditions in your home. Each plan includes a list of materials which will enable you to go to your local supplier (lumber yard, etc.) and order everything that is needed to complete the project. Detailed dimensions are shown on the drawing so that all lumber can be pre-cut by your supplier.

Before you get started, the following steps should be taken to insure the best results:

1. If your project is an addition to the exterior of your home, check with your municipal building department to make certain that the project does not violate any setback require- ments for your lot. Often exterior construction projects require a building permit. It can be obtained from your municipal building department.

2. If the project requires financing, show the plan to your local bank or savings and loan association with an estimate of construction costs based on material costs and contractor's fee. Also check your mortgage for an open-end clause that will permit you to re-borrow against the original principal.

3. You may wish to construct the project yourself but if electrical, plumbing or heating jobs are involved, it is strongly advised that you have this work done by contractors in these trades. Check with your local building department. The building code may require inspection approval before any cover-up work can be completed.

4. Be sure to check out problems that may be caused by the addition of an improvement, such as overloaded electric circuits, the need for relocating outlets, etc.

5. Order material in advance, assembling everything you need before you begin work on your project. Even standard materials are not always stocked and may need to be ordered for you. Special orders can take up to 8 weeks for delivery.

Best wishes for a successful undertaking. When your project is completed, we would like to have a snapshot of it and hear from you about what you liked about ahead of time in my plan.

Cordially,

Augustus Suglia,
Architect

WORKSHOPS & GARDEN SHEDS

(also for tools, cordwood or small dogs)

1.

BAY WINDOW GREENHOUSE

With lots of garden storage

A-frame greenhouse: If you're into gardening and need a place to store equipment and start plants, this attractive A-frame greenhouse could be the answer.

Plastic roof over plant section allows plenty of sunlight. Work bench is built into opposite side. Greenhouse is 12' wide; 10'2" deep; 7' high.

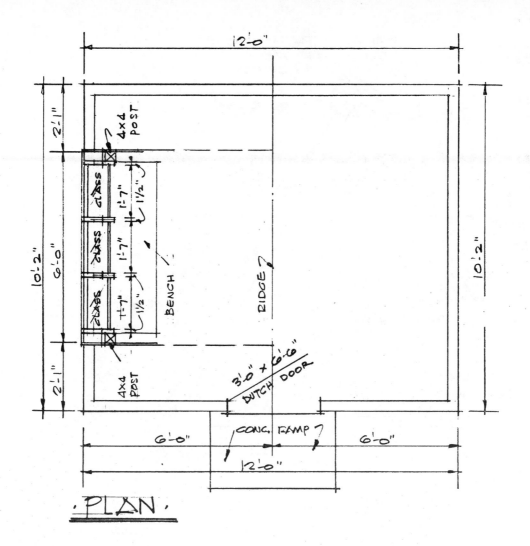

· PLAN ·

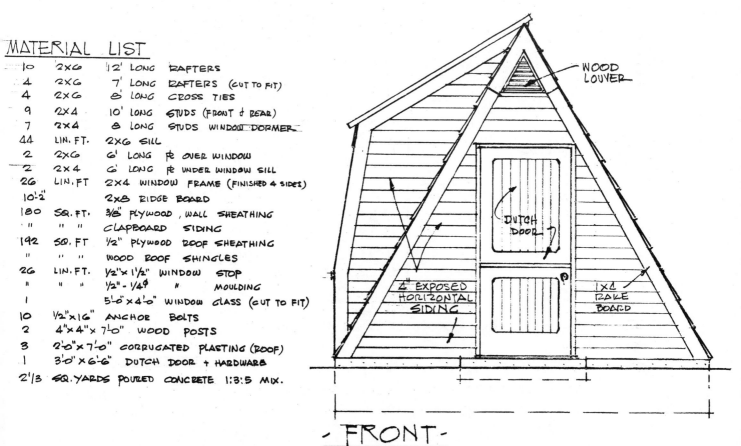

MATERIAL LIST

10	2×6	12' LONG	RAFTERS
4	2×6	7' LONG	RAFTERS (CUT TO FIT)
4	2×6	8' LONG	CROSS TIES
9	2×4	10' LONG	STUDS (FRONT & REAR)
7	2×4	8' LONG	STUDS WINDOW DORMER
44	LIN. FT.	2×6 SILL	
2	2×6	6' LONG	⅊ OVER WINDOW
2	2×4	6' LONG	⅊ UNDER WINDOW SILL
26	LIN. FT	2×4 WINDOW FRAME (FINISHED 4 SIDES)	
		10'-2"	2×8 RIDGE BOARD
180	SQ. FT.	⅜ PLYWOOD, WALL SHEATHING	
"	" "	CLAPBOARD SIDING	
192	SQ. FT	½" PLYWOOD ROOF SHEATHING	
"	" "	WOOD ROOF SHINGLES	
26	LIN. FT.	½"× 1½" WINDOW STOP	
"	" "	½" - 1¼" " MOULDING	
1		5'-0"×4'-0" WINDOW GLASS (CUT TO FIT)	
10	½"×16"	ANCHOR BOLTS	
2	4"×4"×7'-0"	WOOD POSTS	
3	2'-0"×7'-0"	CORRUGATED PLASTIC (ROOF)	
1	3'-0"×6'-6"	DUTCH DOOR + HARDWARE	
2⅓ SQ. YARDS POURED CONCRETE 1:3:5 MIX.			

· FRONT ·

9

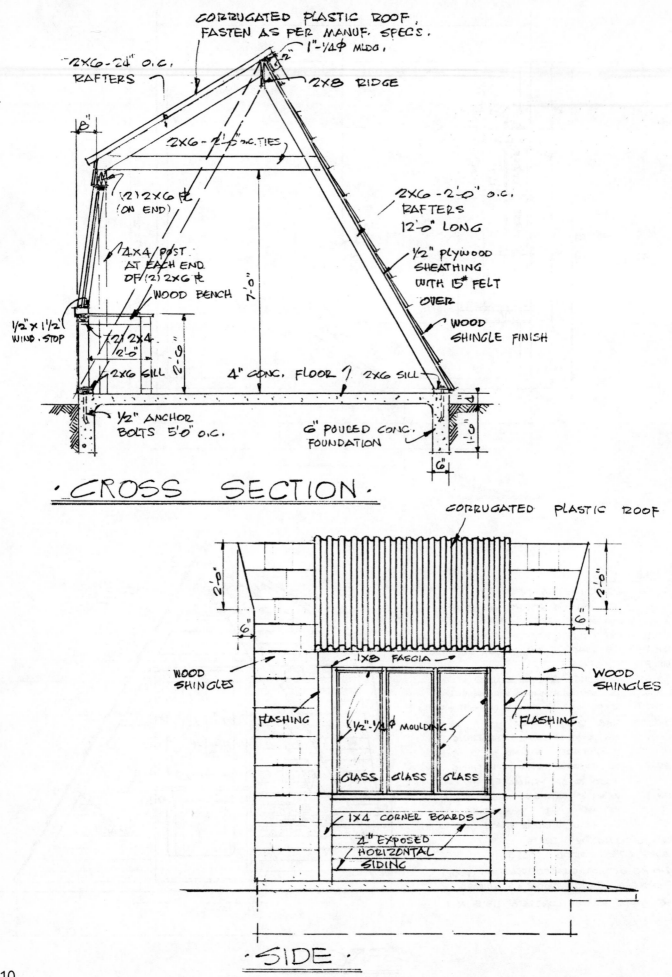

CORRUGATED PLASTIC ROOF,
FASTEN AS PER MANUF. SPECS.
1"-1/4 ∅ MLDG.

2X6 - 24" O.C.
RAFTERS

2X8 RIDGE

2X6 - 2'-0" O.C. TIES

(2) 2X6 R.
(ON END)

2X6 - 2'-0" O.C.
RAFTERS
12'-0" LONG

1X4 POST
AT EACH END
OF (2) 2X6 R.

WOOD BENCH

1/2" plywood
SHEATHING
WITH 15# FELT
OVER

7'-0"

WOOD
SHINGLE FINISH

1/2" X 1 1/2"
WIND. STOP

(2) 2X4
2'-0"

2X6 SILL

4" CONC. FLOOR

2X6 SILL

1/2" ANCHOR
BOLTS 5'-0" O.C.

6" POURED CONC.
FOUNDATION

6"

· CROSS SECTION ·

CORRUGATED PLASTIC ROOF

2'-0"

6"

2'-0"

6"

WOOD
SHINGLES

1X8 FASCIA

WOOD
SHINGLES

FLASHING

1/2"-1/4 ∅ MOULDING

FLASHING

GLASS   GLASS   GLASS

1X4 CORNER BOARDS

4" EXPOSED
HORIZONTAL
SIDING

· SIDE ·

10

DORMERED A-FRAME

With clapboard siding and a shingled roof

Capital 'A': A 7-foot A frame is the heart of a solarium-storage shed. Corrugated plastic panels make an economical sun roof, wood parts are stained or painted and shingles cover the frame. Building plans show shelves in 12x10-foot shed.

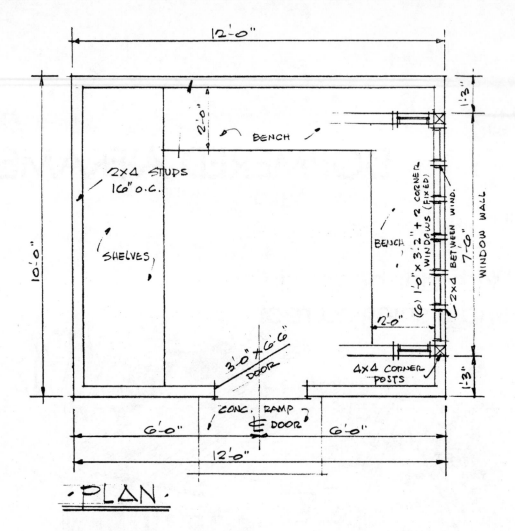

·PLAN·

Dimensions and labels on plan:
- 12'-0"
- 10'-0"
- 2×4 STUDS 16" O.C.
- SHELVES
- 2'-0"
- BENCH
- BENCH
- 1'-3"
- 7'-6"
- 1'-3"
- WINDOW WALL
- 2×4 BETWEEN WIND.
- (6) 1'-0" × 3'-2" + 2 CORNER WINDOWS (FIXED)
- 2'-0"
- 3'-0" × 6'-6" DOOR
- 4×4 CORNER POSTS
- CONC. RAMP & DOOR
- 6'-0"
- 6'-0"
- 12'-0"

MATERIAL LIST

10	2×6	12' LONG	RAFTERS
7	2×4	7' LONG	RAFTERS
8	2×6	8' LONG	CROSS TIES
33	2×4	8' LONG	STUDS
52	LIN·FT.	BENCH FRAMING (2×4)	
44	LIN·FT.	2×6 SILL	
2	2×6	7'-6" WINDOW HEADER	
1	1/2"-4×8	PLYWOOD FOR RAFTER GUSSET	
144	SQ.FT	1/2" PLYWOOD ROOF SHEATHING	
144	SQ.FT	WOOD SHINGLES FOR ROOF	
180	SQ.FT	1/2" PLYWOOD WALL SHEATHING	
180	SQ.FT	CLAPBOARD SIDING	
1	2×8	12' LONG RIDGE BOARD	
2	4×4	6'-6" LONG CORNER POSTS	
64	LIN.FT.	1/2" × 1 1/2" WINDOW STOP	
1		3'-0" × 6'-6" EXTERIOR DOOR & HARDWARE	
8		1'-0" × 3'-2" WINDOW GLASS	
10		1/2" × 10" ANCHOR BOLTS	
44	SQ.FT.	3/4" PLYWOOD BENCH TOP	

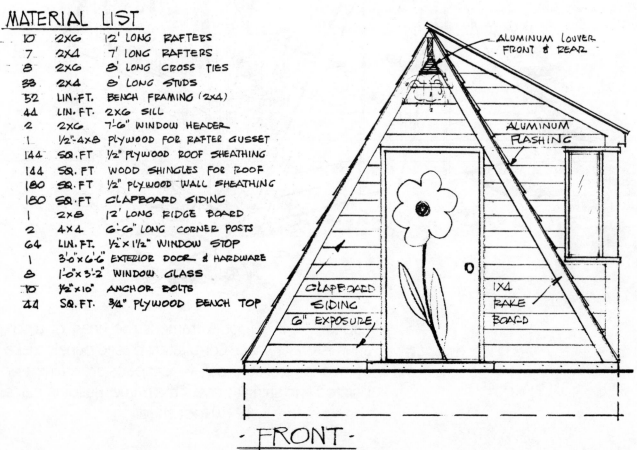

Labels on front elevation:
- ALUMINUM LOUVER FRONT & REAR
- ALUMINUM FLASHING
- CLAPBOARD SIDING 6" EXPOSURE
- 1×4 RAKE BOARD

· FRONT ·

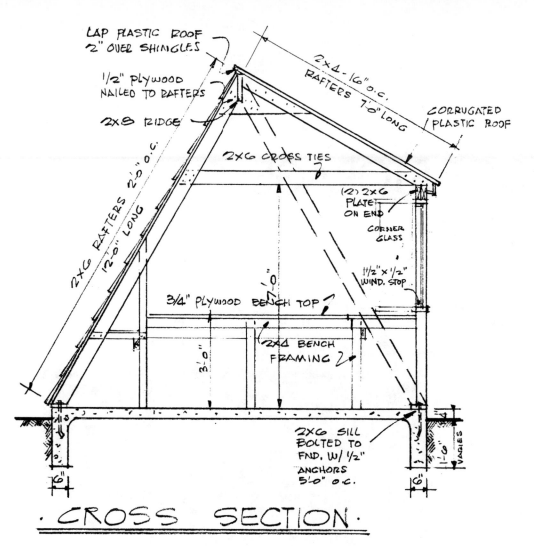

LAP PLASTIC ROOF 2" OVER SHINGLES

1/2" PLYWOOD NAILED TO RAFTERS

2X8 RIDGE

2X6 RAFTERS 2'6" O.C.

2X6 RAFTERS 12'-0" LONG

2X4 - 16" O.C. RAFTERS 7'0" LONG

CORRUGATED PLASTIC ROOF

2X6 CROSS TIES

(2) 2X6 PLATE ON END

CORNER GLASS

1 1/2" X 1/2" WIND. STOP

3/4" PLYWOOD BENCH TOP

2X4 BENCH FRAMING

3'-0"

2X6 SILL BOLTED TO FND. W/ 1/2" ANCHORS 5'-0" O.C.

VARIES

6"

6"

· CROSS SECTION ·

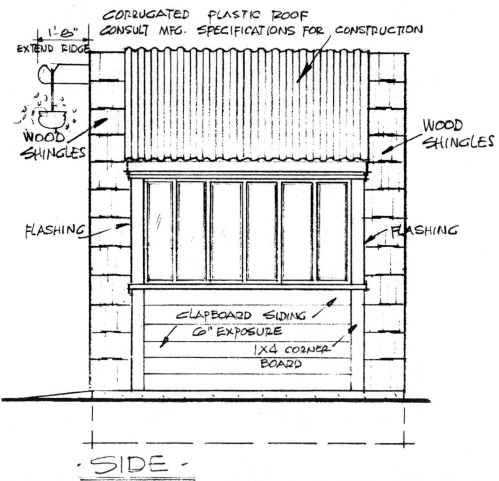

CORRUGATED PLASTIC ROOF
CONSULT MFG. SPECIFICATIONS FOR CONSTRUCTION

1'-8" EXTEND RIDGE

WOOD SHINGLES

WOOD SHINGLES

FLASHING

FLASHING

CLAPBOARD SIDING 6" EXPOSURE

1X4 CORNER BOARD

· SIDE ·

13

3.

SHED ROOF STORAGE

Handy shed can stash outdoor equipment

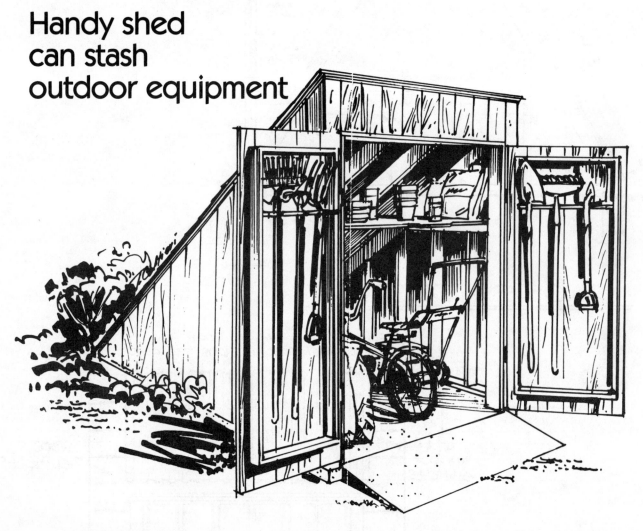

Storage shed plan: If it's so crowded with gardening gear, bicycles, and other outdoor equipment, that you can't use your garage to park your car, it's time for a change. Declutter the garage by building a shed. It's 7 feet wide by 8 feet, 8 inches deep by 8 feet high at front. Two doors swing open to give you full access to supplies. Built-in racks on doors hang gardening tools; shelf across width of shed can hold potting soil, paint cans, other supplies. Ramp at front makes it easy to wheel mower or bicycle in or out.

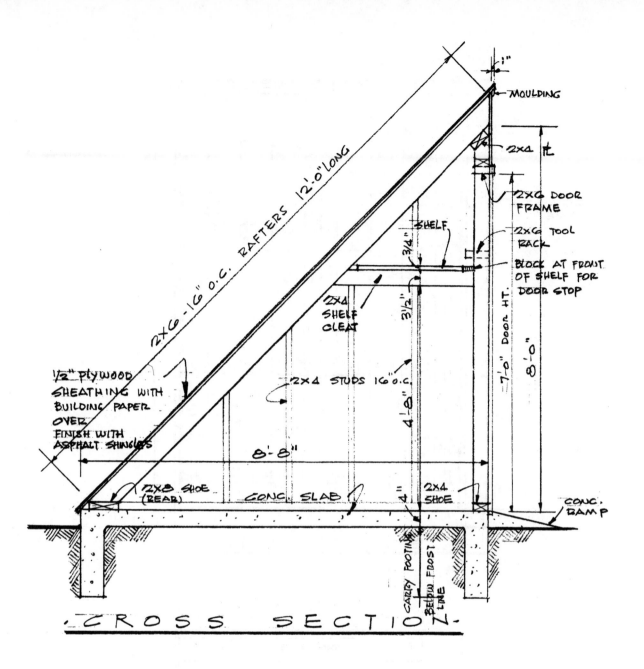

2×6-16" O.C. RAFTERS 12'-0" LONG

½" PLYWOOD
SHEATHING WITH
BUILDING PAPER
OVER
FINISH WITH
ASPHALT SHINGLES

2×4
SHELF
CLEAT

2×4 STUDS 16"O.C.

3/4" SHELF

3½"

4'-8"

MOULDING

2×4

2×6 DOOR
FRAME

2×6 TOOL
RACK

BLOCK AT FRONT
OF SHELF FOR
DOOR STOP

7'-0" DOOR HT.

8'-0"

8'-8"

2×8 SHOE
(REAR)

CONC. SLAB

2×4
SHOE

CARRY FOOTING
BELOW FROST
LINE

CONC.
RAMP

CROSS SECTION

MATERIAL LIST

LOCATION	SIZE	AMOUNT	LIN. FT.
STUDS	2×4	12/8'	96
PLATES & SHOE	2×4	–	34
SHOE @ REAR	2×6	1/7	7
RAFTERS	2×6	5/12	60
DOOR FRAME	2×6	3/8	24
INSIDE DOOR	2×4	6/7'	42
FRAME	2×6	2/3'	6

SHEATHING & FINISHING SQ. FOOTAGE

SIDE WALLS	= 133	SQ. FT.
ROOF	= 86	SQ. FT.

15

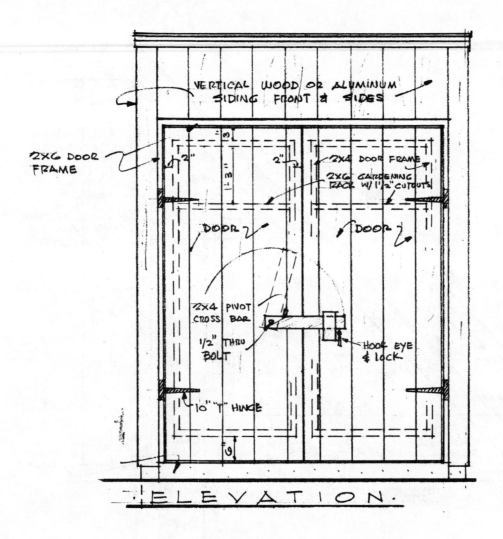

VERTICAL WOOD OR ALUMINUM
SIDING FRONT & SIDES

2X6 DOOR FRAME

2"   3"   2"

2X4 DOOR FRAME

2X6 GARDENING RACK W/ 1½" CUTOUTS

DOOR

DOOR

2X4 PIVOT CROSS BAR

½" THRU BOLT

HOOK EYE & LOCK

10" "T" HINGE

6

. E L E V A T I O N .

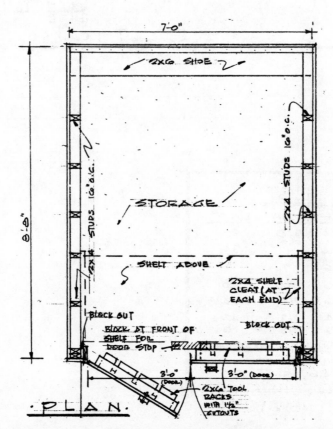

7'-0"

2X6 SHOE

2X4 STUDS 16" O.C.

2X4 STUDS 16" O.C.

8'-0"

STORAGE

SHELF ABOVE

2X4 SHELF CLEAT (AT EACH END)

BLOCK OUT

BLOCK OUT

BLOCK AT FRONT OF SHELF FOR DOOR STOP

3'-0" (DOOR)

3'-0" (DOOR)

2X6 TOOL RACKS WITH 1½" CUTOUTS

. P L A N .

4

BARN SHED

The gambrel roof lends a country feeling to practical storage

Storage shed: Designed to store bicycles, mower and other equipment this 7 by 7 foot shed has a ramp for easy access. Shelves can be added inside for smaller aids or garden supplies. Vinyl siding or aluminum is suggested to keep the shed maintenance-free.

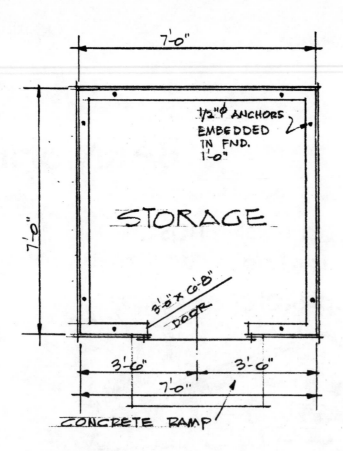

7'-0"

½"∅ ANCHORS
EMBEDDED
IN FND.
1'-0"

STORAGE

3'-0" X 6'-8"
DOOR

7'-0"

3'-6"   3'-6"

7'-0"

CONCRETE RAMP

·PLAN·

FRAMING LUMBER LIST			
LOCATION	SIZE	AMOUNT	LIN. FT.
STUDS	2"X4"	20/7' & 10/2'	90'
PLATES, SILL	2"X4"	12/7'	84'
ROOF RFTS.	2"X4"	10/4'-4"	43'
SIDE RFTS.	2"X4"	10/4'	40'
CEIL. JOISTS	2"X4"	10/7'	70'
COLLAR BMS.	2"X4"	10/3'	30'
LOOKOUTS	2"X4"	10/1'	10'
RIDGE	2"X6"	1/7'	7'
DOOR	3'0"x6'8"	1	—

SHEATHING & FINISHING
SIDE WALLS 3/8" PLYWOOD = 162 SQ.FT.
ROOF   ½" PLYWOOD = 112 SQ.FT.

REQUIRED CONCRETE IN CUBIC YARDS
= 1.15

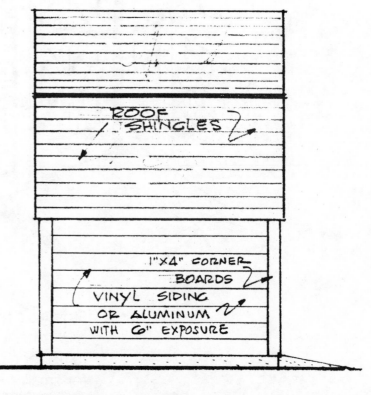

ROOF
SHINGLES

1"X4" CORNER
BOARDS

VINYL SIDING
OR ALUMINUM
WITH 6" EXPOSURE

·SIDE ELEVATION·

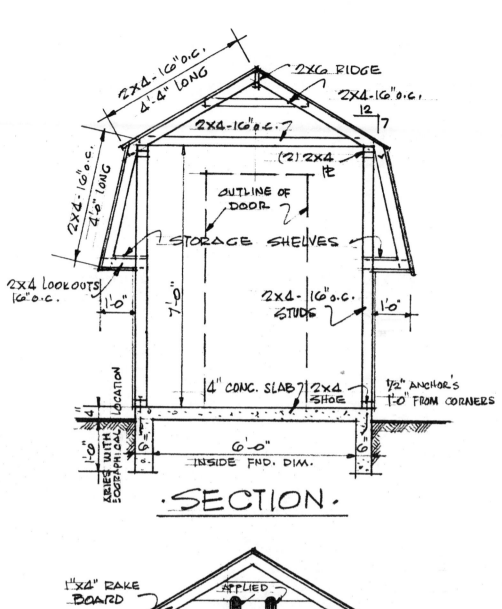

2X4-16"o.c.
4'-4" LONG

2X6 RIDGE

2X4-16"o.c.

2X4-16"o.c.

2X4-16"o.c.

12
7

(2) 2X4

2X4-16"o.c.
4'-6" LONG

OUTLINE OF DOOR

STORAGE SHELVES

12

2X4 LOOKOUTS
16"o.c.

1'-0"

7'-0"

2X4-16"o.c.
STUDS

1'-0"

4" CONC. SLAB

2X4 SHOE

1/2" ANCHOR'S
1'-0" FROM CORNERS

VARIES WITH GEOGRAPHICAL LOCATION

4"

1'-0"

6"

6'-0"
INSIDE FND. DIM.

6"

·SECTION·

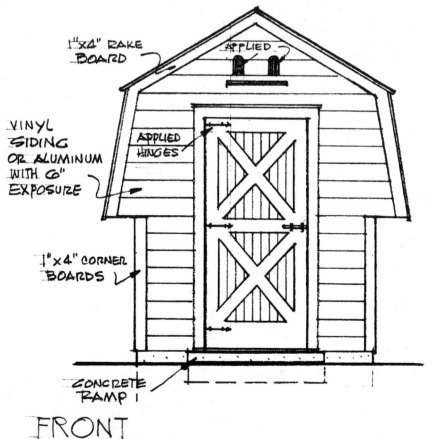

1"X4" RAKE BOARD

APPLIED

VINYL SIDING OR ALUMINUM WITH 6" EXPOSURE

APPLIED HINGES

1"X4" CORNER BOARDS

CONCRETE RAMP

FRONT

5.

WOODSHED

Keep your fuel dry, accessible, and neatly stacked

This narrow shed can be built against property line for log and garden tool storage. Logs are protected from weather and canvas drop can be added for extra protection. Flanking closets will hold garden tools, fertilizers and flammable materials. Unit can be locked to keep children out. Shed is built on concrete slab above ground level. Exterior grooved plywood can be stained or painted. Unit is 11'2" wide.

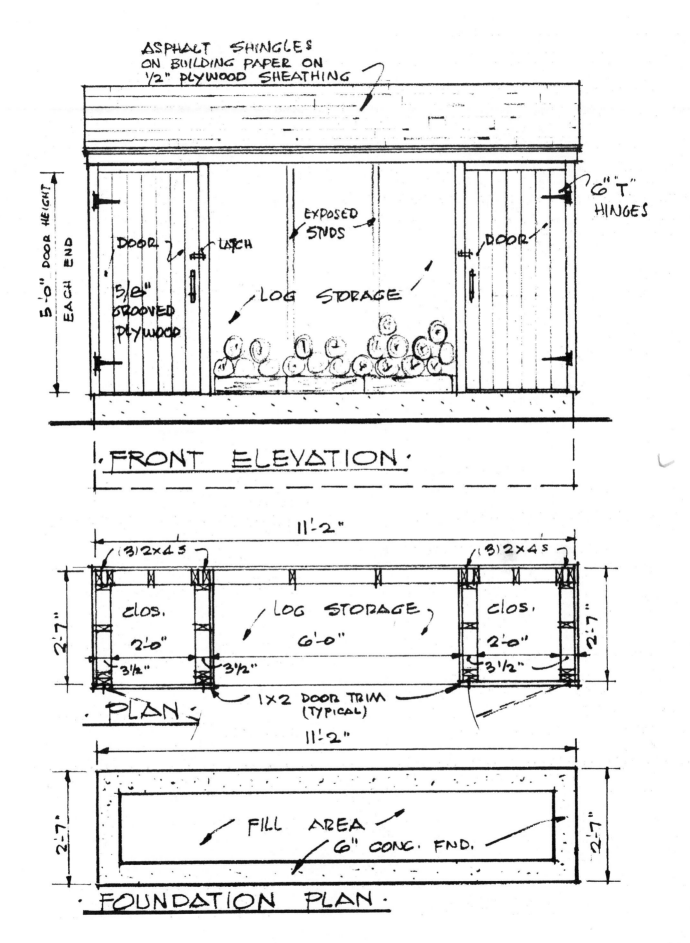

ASPHALT SHINGLES
ON BUILDING PAPER ON
1/2" PLYWOOD SHEATHING

6" "T"
HINGES

5'-0" DOOR HEIGHT
EACH END

DOOR

LATCH

EXPOSED
5TDS

DOOR

5/8"
GROOVED
PLYWOOD

LOG STORAGE

· FRONT ELEVATION ·

11'-2"

(3) 2×4 s

(3) 2×4 s

2'-7"

CLOS.

2'-0"

LOG STORAGE

6'-0"

CLOS.

2'-0"

2'-7"

3 1/2"

3 1/2"

3 1/2"

· PLAN ·

1×2 DOOR TRIM
(TYPICAL)

11'-2"

2'-7"

FILL AREA

6" CONC. FND.

2'-7"

FOUNDATION PLAN ·

21

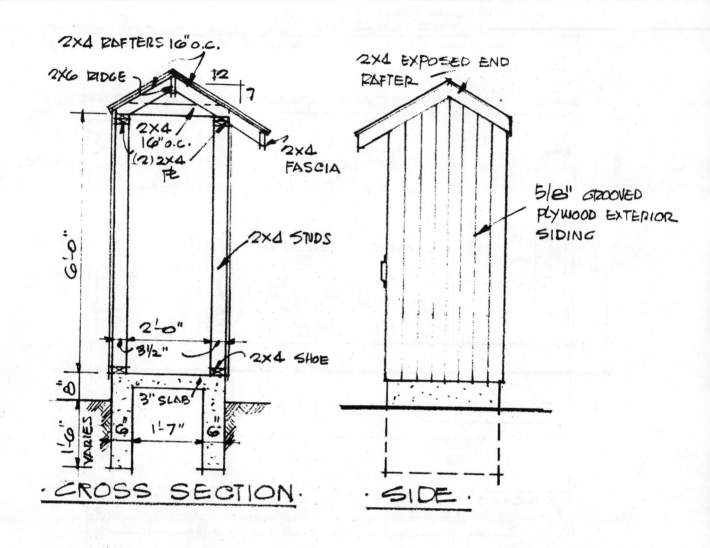

2X4 RAFTERS 16"O.C.

2X6 RIDGE

↑2
7

2X4 EXPOSED END RAFTER

2X4
16"O.C.

(2)2X4
PL

2X4
FASCIA

2X4 STUDS

5/8" GROOVED PLYWOOD EXTERIOR SIDING

6'-0"

2'-0"

3½"

2X4 SHOE

8"

3" SLAB

1'-7"

VARIES

6"

6"

1'-0"

· CROSS SECTION ·

· SIDE ·

MATERIAL LIST

28	2X4/6'-0"	STUDS
9	2X4/2'-7"	RAFTER TIES
9	2X4/4'-0"	RAFTERS (CUT TO FIT)
1	2X6/11'-2"	RIDGE BOARD
77 LIN. FT. 2X4		PLATES TOP & BOTTOM
45 SQ. FT.	ROOFING MATERIALS	
122 SQ. FT. 5/8"	VERTICAL GROOVED PLYWOOD SIDING	

COOKING CENTERS

(with lots of workspace and storage)

6.

BARBECUE WITH BELL TOWER

There's built-in storage space too

Stone barbecue: This impressive barbecue is marvelously well-organized for the outdoor chef. It has two redwood counters—one at left, the other at right. Under each, there is storage space for supplies or trash cans. Wood roof shelters grill and the chef. Note tower with bell to signal that dinner is served. Unit is 10'10'' wide; 3'8'' deep (center), 2' deep (sides), 2'6'' at counters and grill; 8' at chimney.

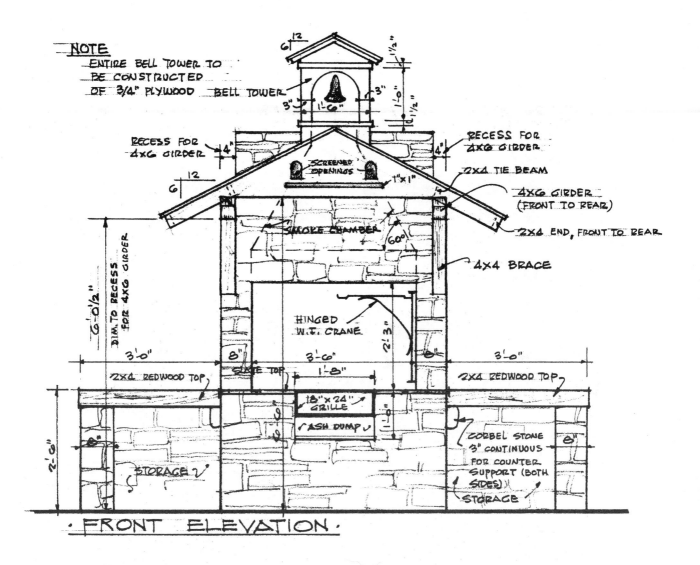

NOTE
ENTIRE BELL TOWER TO
BE CONSTRUCTED
OF 3/4" PLYWOOD   BELL TOWER

6 | 12

1½"

3"   1'-0"   3"

1'-0"

RECESS FOR
4x6 GIRDER   4"

6 | 12

RECESS FOR
4x6 GIRDER   4"

2x4 TIE BEAM

4x6 GIRDER
(FRONT TO REAR)

2x4 END, FRONT TO REAR

SCREENED
OPENINGS   1"x1"

4x4 BRACE

SMOKE CHAMBER

60°

6'-0½"

DIM. TO RECESS
FOR 4x6 GIRDER

HINGED
W.I. CRANE

2'-3"

3'-0"   8"   3'-6"   8"   3'-0"

2x4 REDWOOD TOP   SLATE TOP   2x4 REDWOOD TOP

1'-8"

18" x 24"
GRILLE

ASH DUMP

CORBEL STONE
3" CONTINUOUS
FOR COUNTER
SUPPORT (BOTH
SIDES)
STORAGE

2'-6"

STORAGE

· FRONT ELEVATION ·

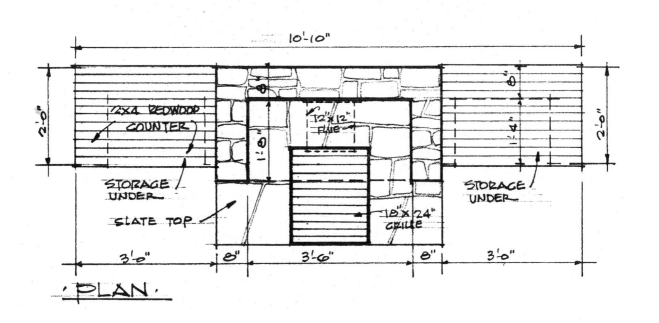

10'-10"

2'-0"

2x4 REDWOOD
COUNTER

12" x 12"
FLUE

2'-0"

STORAGE
UNDER

SLATE TOP

18" x 24"
GRILLE

STORAGE
UNDER

3'-0"   8"   3'-6"   8"   3'-0"

· PLAN ·

25

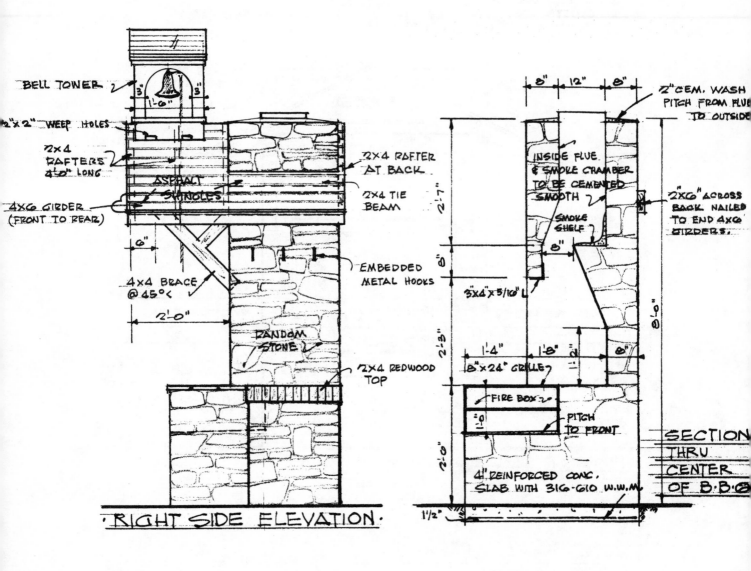

BELL TOWER

2"x2" WEEP HOLES

2x4 RAFTERS 4'-0" LONG

ASPHALT SHINGLES

4x6 GIRDER (FRONT TO REAR)

4x4 BRACE @ 45°<

2'-0"

RANDOM STONE

2x4 RAFTER AT BACK

2x4 TIE BEAM

EMBEDDED METAL HOOKS

2x4 REDWOOD TOP

·RIGHT SIDE ELEVATION·

8" 12" 8"

2"CEM. WASH PITCH FROM FLUE TO OUTSIDE

INSIDE FLUE & SMOKE CHAMBER TO BE CEMENTED SMOOTH

SMOKE SHELF

2"x6" ACROSS BACK NAILED TO END 4x6 GIRDERS.

3"x4"x5/16" L

8"

1'-4" 1'-8" 8"

18"x24" GRILLE

FIRE BOX

PITCH TO FRONT

4" REINFORCED CONC. SLAB WITH 316-610 W.W.M.

SECTION THRU CENTER OF B.B.Q

1 1/2"

·MATERIAL LIST·B.B.Q.·

100 CU. FT. STONE
22 CU. FT. MORTAR
1 18"x24" GRILLE
1 18"x24" GRATE
1 3"x4"x5/16" LINTEL 4'-0" LONG
16 2"x4"x6'-0" REDWOOD COUNTER
1 1'-4"x1'-4" HINGED W.I. CRANE

·FRAMING LUMBER LIST (ROOF)

LOCATION	SIZE	AMOUNT	LIN.FT
RAFTERS	2x4	8/4'-0"	32
MISC.	2x4	—	18
GIRDER	4x6	2/4'-6"	9
BRACE	4x4	—	7

ROOFING 1/2" PLYWOOD 26 SQ. FT.
BELL TOWER 3/4" PLYWOOD 14 SQ. FT.

26

7.

WISHING WELL
COOKOUT CENTER

It's a Bar-B-Q!
with a
shingled roof

If you think this is a decorative do-nothing wishing well for the yard, look again. It's a cookout center for the chef. Pre-fabricated Bar-B-Q unit has cooking grate, firebox and ash dump. Slate counter offers work space. Inverted bucket shields light bulb. Well, 3 feet square, is 6 feet, 6 inches high.

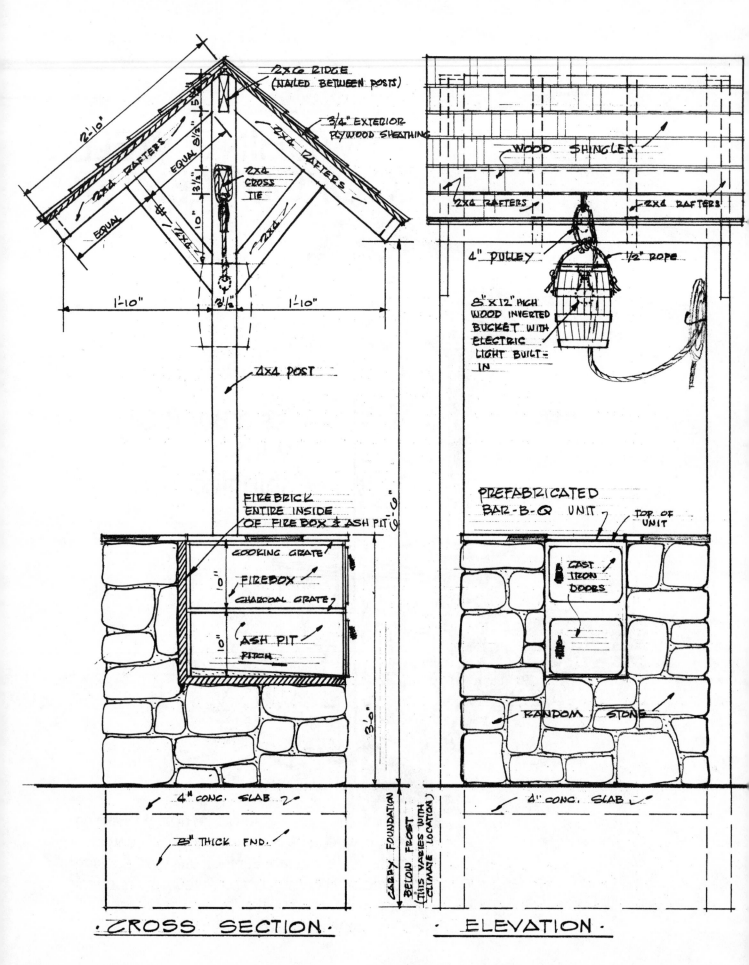

2x6 RIDGE
(NAILED BETWEEN POSTS)

3/4" EXTERIOR
PLYWOOD SHEATHING

2'-10"

2x4 RAFTERS

2x4 RAFTERS

2x4
CROSS
TIE

EQUAL

EQUAL

3 1/2

5

8 1/2

3 1/2

4"

10"

2x4

2x4

3 1/2

1'-10"   1'-10"

2x4 POST

FIREBRICK
ENTIRE INSIDE
OF FIRE BOX & ASH PIT

6'-0"

COOKING GRATE
FIREBOX
CHARCOAL GRATE

10"

10"

ASH PIT
PITCH

3'-0"

4" CONC. SLAB

8" THICK FND.

CARRY FOUNDATION
BELOW FROST
(THIS VARIES WITH
CLIMATE LOCATION)

· CROSS SECTION ·

WOOD SHINGLES

2x4 RAFTERS   2x4 RAFTERS

4" PULLEY   1/2" ROPE

8"x12" HIGH
WOOD INVERTED
BUCKET WITH
ELECTRIC
LIGHT BUILT-
IN

PREFABRICATED
BAR-B-Q UNIT

TOP OF
UNIT

CAST
IRON
DOORS

RANDOM STONE

4" CONC. SLAB

· ELEVATION ·

28

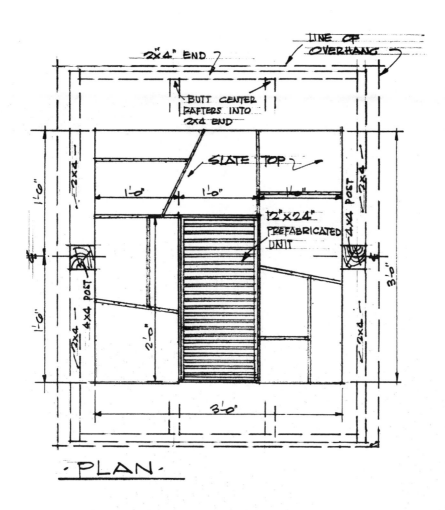

· PLAN ·

MATERIAL LIST

24	CU. FT. RANDOM STONE
6	" " MORTAR
	8"x16" CONC. BLOCKS SET IN
	1:3 P.C. MORTAR (FOUNDATION)
11	2X4 / 3'-0" LONG (CUT TO FIT)
2	2X4 / 3'-0" RAFTER ENDS
1	2X6 / 3'-0" RIDGE
2	3/4" x 4'-0" PLYWOOD SHEATHING
48	SQ. FT. WOOD ROOF SHINGLES
2	4X4 / 2'-6" WOOD POSTS
7	SQ. FT. SLATE FOR COUNTER
1	PREFABRICATE B-F-Q. UNIT
1	BUCKET, PULLEY & 1/2" ROPE
10	SQ. FT.
	FIRE BRICK

8.

CORNER COOKOUT CENTER

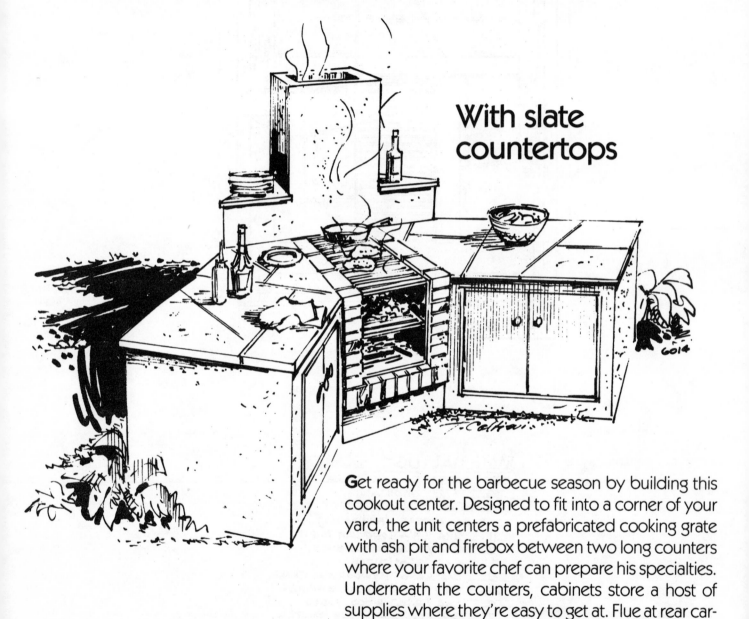

With slate countertops

Get ready for the barbecue season by building this cookout center. Designed to fit into a corner of your yard, the unit centers a prefabricated cooking grate with ash pit and firebox between two long counters where your favorite chef can prepare his specialties. Underneath the counters, cabinets store a host of supplies where they're easy to get at. Flue at rear carries smoke from the firebox away from the cooking area.

Use slate on the counter tops for a touch of color plus easy maintenance. Build unit of brick or, for economy, use concrete blocks with stucco finish. Unit is 3 feet high; 8 feet long from center rear to each side.

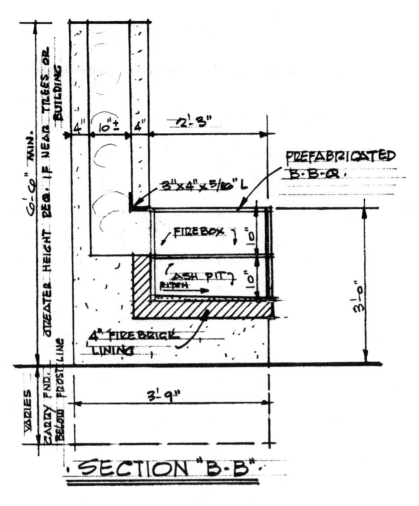

6'-0" MIN.

GREATER HEIGHT REQ. IF NEAR TREES OR BUILDING

CARRY FND. BELOW FROST LINE

VARIES

4" — 10"± — 4" — 2'-3"

PREFABRICATED B.B.Q.

3"x4"x5/16" L

FIREBOX — 10"

ASH PIT — 10"
PITCH

3'-0"

4" FIREBRICK LINING

3'-9"

SECTION "B-B"

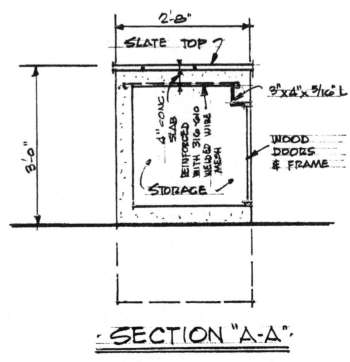

2'-8"

SLATE TOP

4" CONC. SLAB
REINFORCED WITH 316-610 WELDED WIRE MESH

3"x4"x5/16" L

WOOD DOORS & FRAME

3'-0"

STORAGE

SECTION "A-A"

MATERIAL LIST

100	SQ. FT. OF 4"x8"x16" CONC. BLOCKS
1	BAR-B-Q. UNIT 15"x 27"x 20" HIGH
19	SQ. FT. OF FIREBRICKS
2	STEEL LINTELS 3"x4"x5/16"/3'-8" LONG.
1	" LINTEL " " " /1'-9" "
51	SQ. FT. OF 4"x8"x16" CONC. BLOCKS FOR FND. (1'-6" DEPTH SHOWN)
2	3'-8" x 2'-10" WELDED WIRE MESH #316-610
30	SQ. FT. ½" SLATE (COUNTER TOP)

WOOD

21	LIN. FT 3/4"x 2½" DOOR FRAME
2	2'x 3' EXTERIOR PLYWOOD 3/4" CUT TO FIT (4 DOORS)
2	PAIR HINGES
2	PULL KNOBS

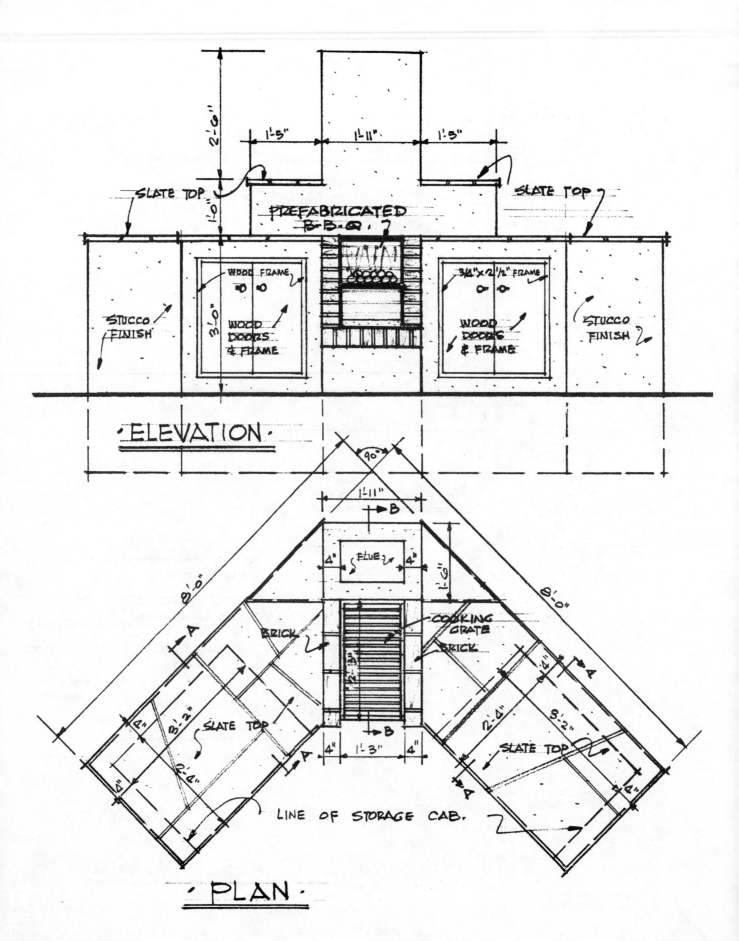

ELEVATION

SLATE TOP

SLATE TOP

PREFABRICATED B-B-Q.

2'-6"

1'-5"   1'-11"   1'-5"

1'-0"

STUCCO FINISH

WOOD FRAME

WOOD DOORS & FRAME

3'-0"

3/4" x 2 1/2" FRAME

WOOD DOORS & FRAME

STUCCO FINISH

PLAN

90°

1'-11"

B

4"   FLUE   4"

1'-6"

8'-0"

8'-0"

A

BRICK

COOKING GRATE

BRICK

4"   4"

3'-2"

SLATE TOP

2'-3"

2'-4"

3'-2"

SLATE TOP

4"

4"   1'-3"   4"

A   B

A

4"

A

LINE OF STORAGE CAB.

9

BARBECUE PLUS

With an asphalt-shingled roof

Equip the yard for summer and storage with a combination barbecue and shed built under one roof. Shed has two storage areas with doors opening on each side. Redwood work counter is handy to the barbecue, which is built of concrete block for economy. Barbecue-shed unit is 6'6'' wide, 5'5'' deep; 6'4'' high.

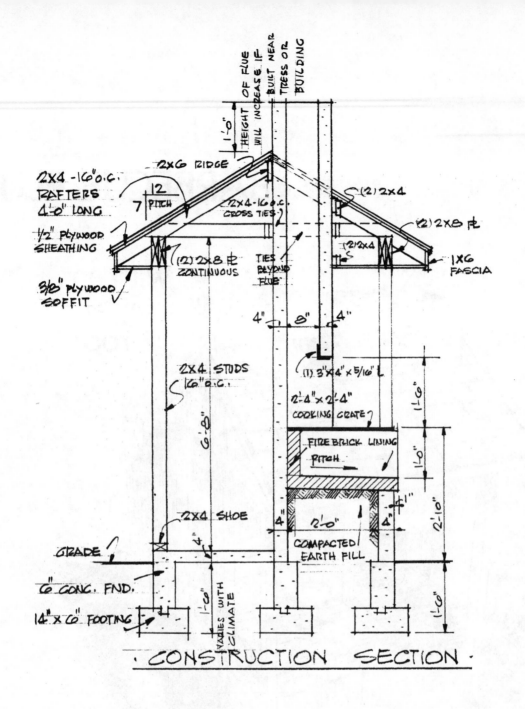

- CONSTRUCTION SECTION -

Labels within drawing:

HEIGHT OF FLUE WILL INCREASE IF BUILT NEAR TREES OR BUILDING

1'-0"

2X6 RIDGE

2X4 -16" O.C. RAFTERS 4'-0" LONG

7 / 12 PITCH

1/2" PLYWOOD SHEATHING

2X4-16" O.C. CROSS TIES

(2) 2X4

(2) 2X8 FL

TIES BEYOND FLUE

(2) 2X4

1X6 FASCIA

3/8" PLYWOOD SOFFIT

(2) 2X8 FL CONTINUOUS

4" 8" 4"

2X4 STUDS 16" O.C.

(1) 3"X4" X 5/16" L

6'-8"

1'-0"

2'-4" X 2'-4" COOKING GRATE

FIREBRICK LINING PITCH

1'-0"

2X4 SHOE

4" 4"

2'-0"

±1"

2'-10"

GRADE

COMPACTED EARTH FILL

6" CONC. FND.

1'-0" VARIES WITH CLIMATE

14" X 6" FOOTING

1'-0"

- MATERIAL LIST -

14	CU. FT.	POURED CONC. FOR FOOTING
27	SQ. FT.	OF 6" CONC. BLOCKS FOR FND.
108	SQ. FT.	OF 4"X8"X16" CONC. BLOCKS, B-B-Q.
7	SQ. FT.	OF 4"X8"X8" " " " "
12	SQ. FT.	OF FIREBRICK, B-B-Q.

WOOD

12	2X4	RAFTERS, 4'-0" LONG
1	2X6	RIDGE, 7'-0" LONG
6	2X4	CROSS TIES 5'-5" LONG
6	4X4	POSTS 6'-0" LONG
10	2X4	STUDS 6'-0" LONG
36	LIN. FT.	2X4 SHOE & MISC.

4	2X8	PLATE, 7'-0" LONG
63	SQ. FT.	1/2" PLYWOOD, ROOF SHEATHING & COUNTER
56	SQ. FT.	ASPHALT SHINGLES, ROOF
8	SQ. FT	2X6 REDWOOD COUNTER
64	SQ. FT.	WOOD SIDING
2	DOORS	2'-0" X 6'-0"
2	CAB. DOORS	14" X 27"
64	LIN. FT.	1X6 CORNER BOARS & FASCIA
16	LIN. FT	1X4 RAKE BOARD
1	ROLL	10" ALUM. FLASHING AT CHIMNEY
4	PAIR	DOOR HINGES
4		DOOR PULLS

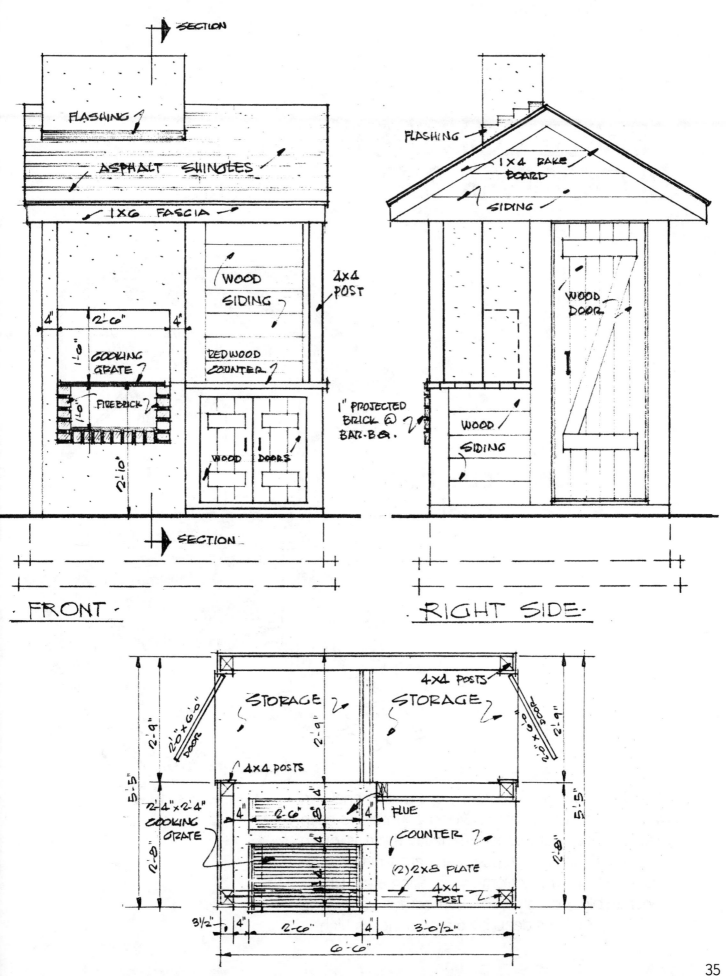

SECTION

FLASHING

ASPHALT SHINGLES

1X6 FASCIA

WOOD SIDING

4X4 POST

4"   2'-6"   4"

1'-0"   COOKING GRATE

1'-0"   FIREBRICK

REDWOOD COUNTER

1" PROJECTED BRICK @ BAR-B-Q.

2'-0"

WOOD DOORS

SECTION

· FRONT ·

FLASHING

1X4 RAKE BOARD

SIDING

WOOD DOOR

WOOD SIDING

· RIGHT SIDE ·

STORAGE

STORAGE

4X4 POSTS

2'-9"

2'-0"x6'-0" DOOR

2'-0"x6'-0" DOOR

4X4 POSTS

2'-9"

2'-9"

5'-5"

5'-5"

2'-4"x2'-4" COOKING GRATE

4"   2'-6"   4"

FLUE

COUNTER

(2)2X8 PLATE

4X4 POST

2'-0"

2'-0"

3½"   4"   2'-0"   4"   3'-0½"

6'-6"

35

10.
SIMPLE CONCRETE BLOCK BAR-B-Q

A barbecue that's extra special

Here's a barbecue plan worthy of a master chef. An awning adds to its charm. Wood counters at each side provide work space. Beneath them is open storage for charcoal, garbage cans, etc. Chimney carries the smoke away from the cooking area. Unit is concrete block construction. Barbecue is 6 feet wide by 2 feet, 3 inches deep by 6 feet, 6 inches high.

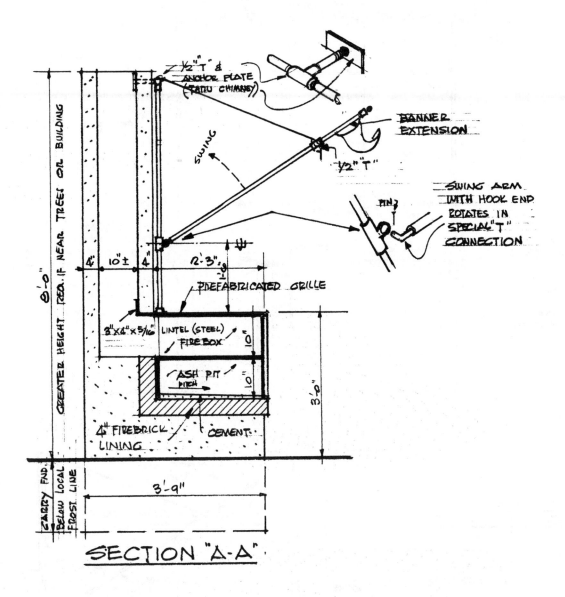

½"T & ANCHOR PLATE (TALLU CHIMNEY)

SWING

BANNER EXTENSION

½"T"

SWING ARM WITH HOOK END ROTATES IN SPECIAL "T" CONNECTION

PIN

GREATER HEIGHT REQ. IF NEAR TREES OR BUILDING

8'-0"

4" 10"± 4"

2'-3"

9"

PREFABRICATED GRILLE

3"x4"x5/16" LINTEL (STEEL) FIREBOX

10"

10"

3'-0"

ASH PIT PITCH

4" FIREBRICK LINING

CEMENT

CARRY FND. BELOW LOCAL FROST LINE

3'-9"

SECTION "A-A"

MATERIAL LIST

76	SQ. FT. OF 4"x8"x16" CONC. BLOCKS
1	BAR-B-Q. UNIT 15"x27"x20" HIGH
19	SQ. FT. OF FIREBRICKS
1	STEEL LINTEL 3"x4"x5/16"/1'-9" LONG
28	SQ. FT. OF 4"x8"x16" CONC. BLOCKS FOR FND. (1'-6" DEPTH SHOWN)
40	LIN. FT. OF 2"x4" FOR COUNTER TOP
32	LIN. FT. OF ½"⌀ GALVANIZED PIPE
2	½"⌀ PIPE ELBOWS
1	½"⌀ SPECIAL "T" ANCHOR & ℞ AT TOP
2	½"⌀ " SWING ARM "T"
2	½"⌀ CIRCULAR BASE ANCHOR
2	½"⌀ "T"
2	½"⌀ HOOK ENDS WITH PINS FOR SWING ARM CONNECTION.
2	½"⌀ ENDS - TOP OF SWING ARMS
24	SQ. FT. OF CANVAS MADE TO FIT PIPE FRAME WITH CANVAS SEAM AND GROMETS AT TOP FOR FASTENING
	REQUIRED AMOUNT OF MORTAR MIX FOR ALL CONCRETE WORK.
6	½"x8" LONG. PLATE ANCHORS

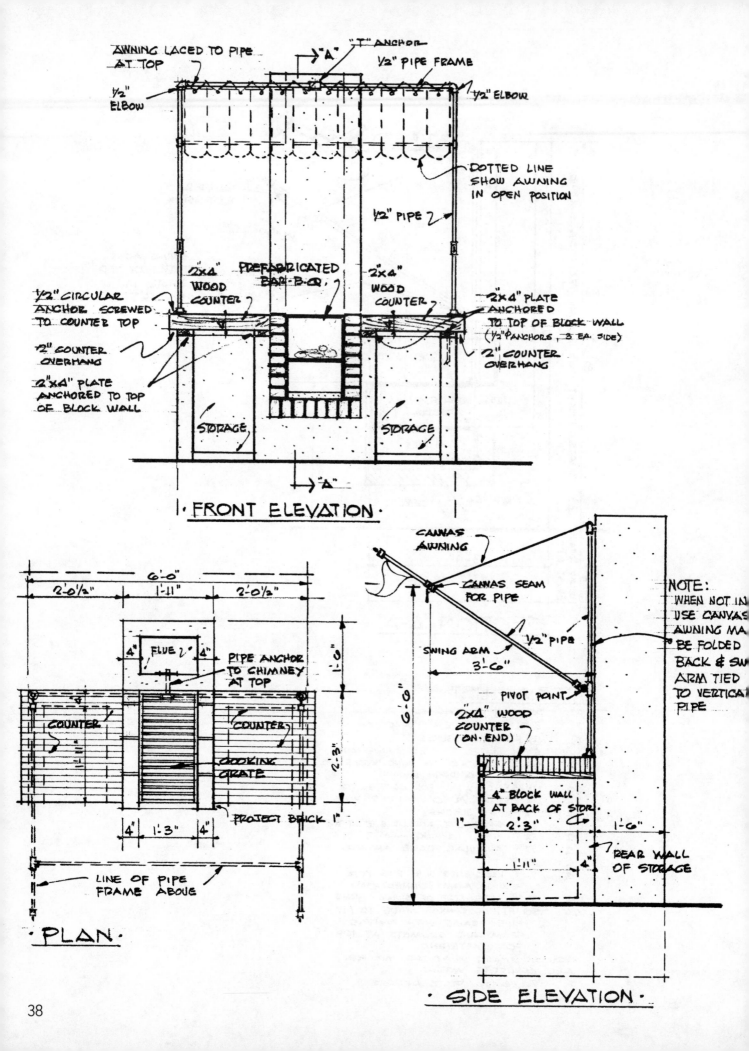

AWNING LACED TO PIPE AT TOP
"T" ANCHOR
½" PIPE FRAME
"A"
½" ELBOW
½" ELBOW
1/2" PIPE
DOTTED LINE SHOW AWNING IN OPEN POSITION
2"x4" WOOD COUNTER
PREFABRICATED BAR-B-Q
2"x4" WOOD COUNTER
2"x4" PLATE ANCHORED TO TOP OF BLOCK WALL (½" ANCHORS, 3 EA. SIDE)
½" CIRCULAR ANCHOR SCREWED TO COUNTER TOP
2" COUNTER OVERHANG
2" COUNTER OVERHANG
2"x4" PLATE ANCHORED TO TOP OF BLOCK WALL
STORAGE
STORAGE
"A"

· FRONT ELEVATION ·

6'-0"
2'-0½"
1'-11"
2'-0½"
4"
FLUE
4"
PIPE ANCHOR TO CHIMNEY AT TOP
1'-0"
COUNTER
COUNTER
2'-3"
COOKING GRATE
4"
1'-3"
4"
PROJECT BRICK 1"
LINE OF PIPE FRAME ABOVE

· PLAN ·

CANVAS AWNING
CANVAS SEAM FOR PIPE
NOTE: WHEN NOT IN USE CANVAS MAY BE FOLDED BACK & SWING ARM TIED TO VERTICAL PIPE
SWING ARM
½" PIPE
3'-6"
6'-0"
PIVOT POINT
2"x4" WOOD COUNTER (ON END)
4" BLOCK WALL AT BACK OF STOR.
2'-3"
1'-6"
1"
1'-11"
4"
REAR WALL OF STORAGE

· SIDE ELEVATION ·

DAYPLACES

(for holding hands and summer celebrations)

11.

SUMMER ROOM

It's all
screened in

Build yourself a 10' x 12' outdoor living room that's screened in so you can enjoy it, but insects can't. Shingle roof is louvered at each end, making a shady, airy summer retreat.

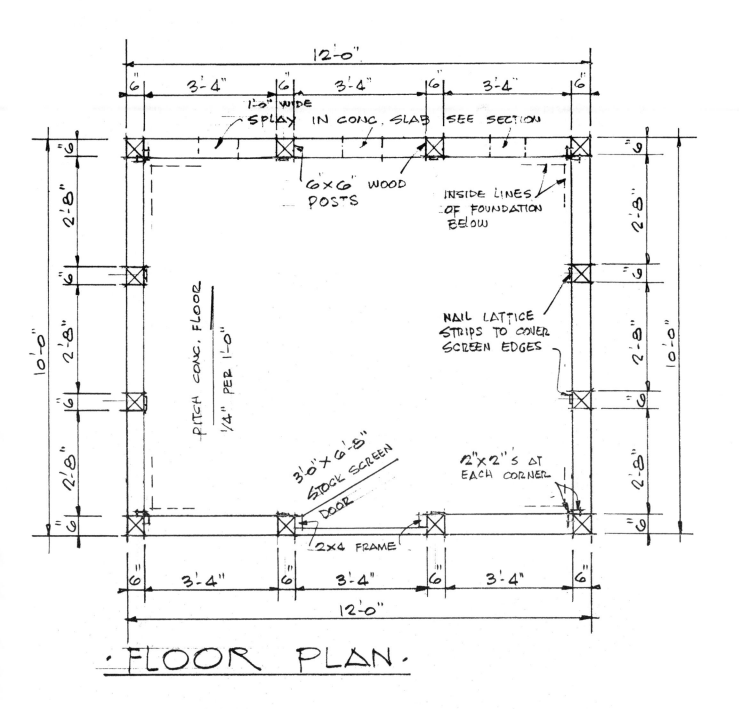

·FLOOR PLAN·

MATERIAL LIST.

12	6"×6"×8'-0" WOOD POSTS		4	2"×6"×12'-0" SILL & RAIL
12	2"×6"×7'-0" RAFTERS		4	2"×6'×10'-0" " " "
10	2"×6"×3'-0" SIDE RAFTERS		6	1/4"×1"×12'-0" LATTICE
4	2"×6"×4'-0" CORNER RAFTERS		6	" " ×10'-0" "
2	2"×6"×8'-0" RAFTER NAILERS		16	" " ×8'-0" "
1	2"×6"×12'-0" RIDGE BOARD		1	3'-0"×6'-8" SCREEN DOOR
6	2"×4"×4'-0" RAFTER TIES		400	SQ.FT. ALUMINUM OR VINYL SCREENING
6	2"×4"×10'-0" " "		2	WOOD LOUVERS (OR ALUMINUM)
6	2"×6"×12'-0" PLATES		185	SQ.FT. 1/2" PLYWOOD SHEATHING (ROOF)
6	2"×6"×10'-0" "		185	" " WOOD SHINGLES
			4.5	SQ.YDS POURED CONCRETE

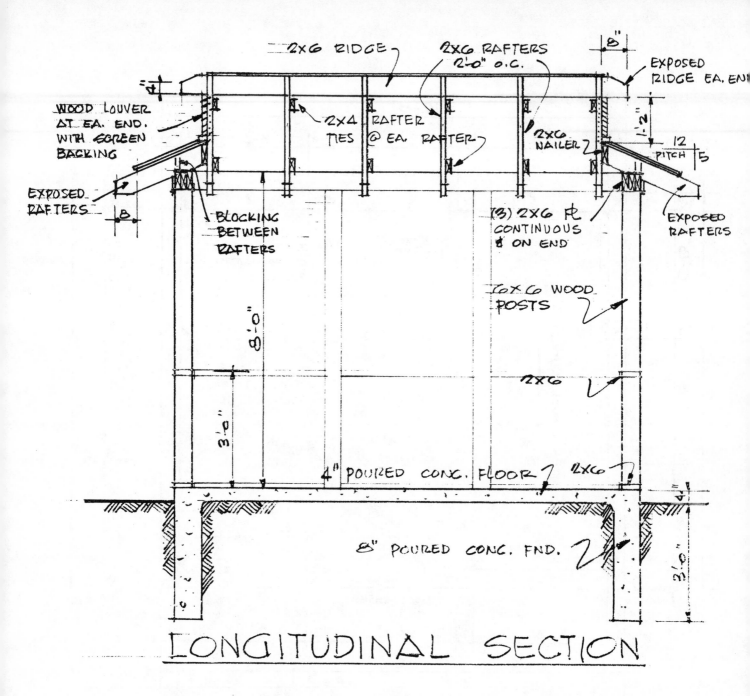

2x6 RIDGE

2x6 RAFTERS 2'-0" O.C.

8"

EXPOSED RIDGE EA. END

WOOD LOUVER AT EA. END. WITH SCREEN BACKING

2x4 RAFTER TIES @ EA. RAFTER

2x6 NAILER

1'-2"

12 PITCH 5

EXPOSED RAFTERS

8"

BLOCKING BETWEEN RAFTERS

EXPOSED RAFTERS

(3) 2x6 PL CONTINUOUS & ON END

6x6 WOOD POSTS

8'-0"

2x6

3'-0"

4" POURED CONC. FLOOR

2x6

8" POURED CONC. FND.

3'-0"

LONGITUDINAL SECTION

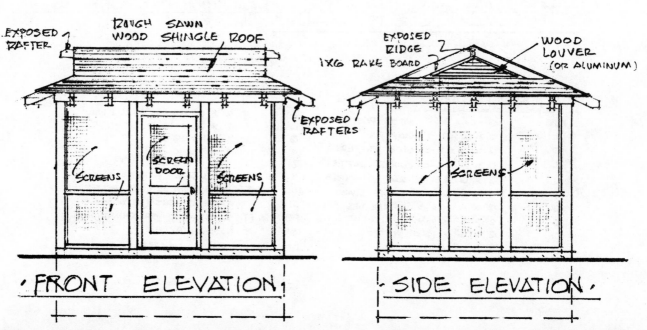

EXPOSED RAFTER

ROUGH SAWN WOOD SHINGLE ROOF

EXPOSED RIDGE

1X6 RAKE BOARD

WOOD LOUVER (OR ALUMINUM)

EXPOSED RAFTERS

SCREENS

SCREEN DOOR

SCREENS

SCREENS

FRONT ELEVATION

SIDE ELEVATION

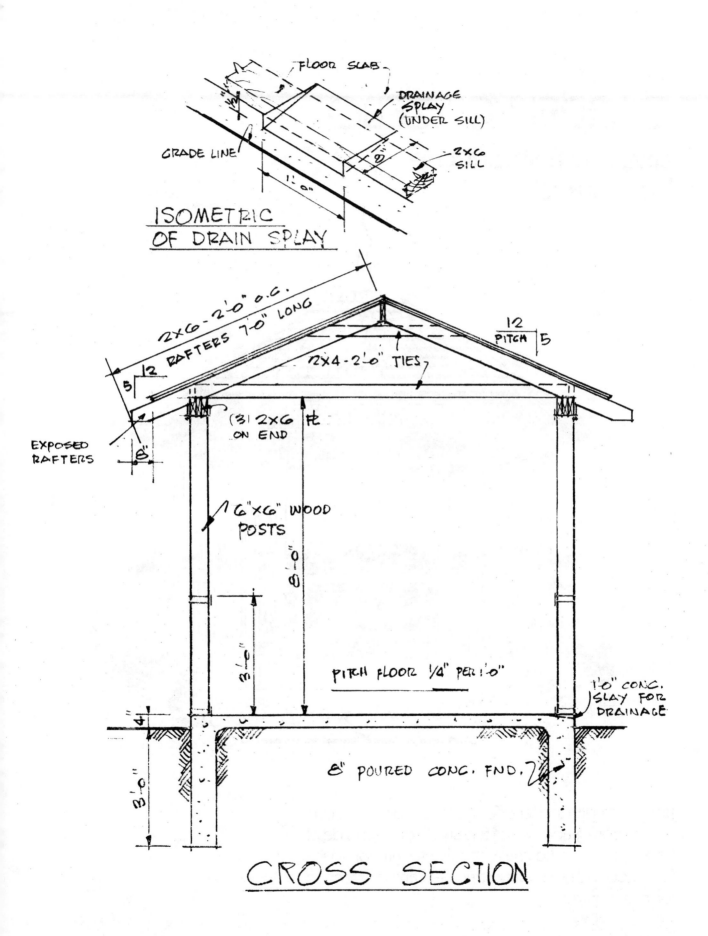

FLOOR SLAB

DRAINAGE
SPLAY
(UNDER SILL)

GRADE LINE

2×6
SILL

1'-0"

ISOMETRIC
OF DRAIN SPLAY

2×6-2'-0" O.C.
RAFTERS 7'-0" LONG

12
PITCH 5

2×4-2'-0" TIES

5 | 12

5 | 12

EXPOSED
RAFTERS

8"

(3) 2×6 PL.
ON END

6"×6" WOOD
POSTS

8'-0"

3'-0"

PITCH FLOOR ¼" PER 1'-0"

1'-0" CONC.
SLAY FOR
DRAINAGE

4"

3'-0"

8" POURED CONC. FND.

CROSS SECTION

12.

GARDEN GAZEBO
Like old-fashioned bandstands

Roofed garden shelter offers year-round shelter. Unit is 7', 7" from grade to roof top and 5' on each side of hexagon. Table and chairs can fit into interior space for outdoor dining. Entire structure can be screened for pest control.

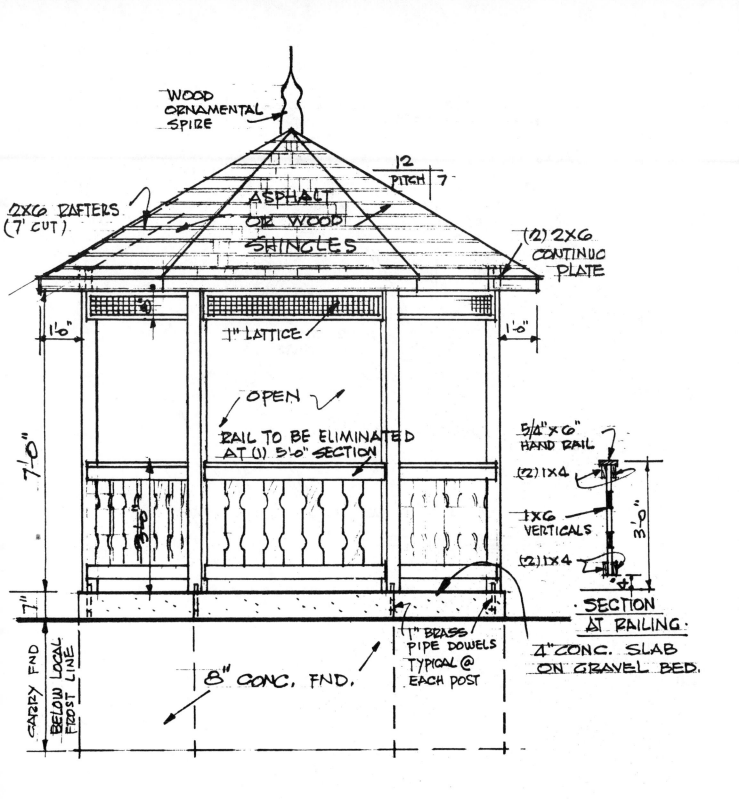

WOOD
ORNAMENTAL
SPIRE

12
PITCH 7

2X6 RAFTERS
(7' CUT)

ASPHALT
OR WOOD
SHINGLES

(2) 2X6
CONTINUO
PLATE

1'0"

1" LATTICE

1'0"

OPEN

RAIL TO BE ELIMINATED
AT (1) 5'0" SECTION

5/4"X 6"
HAND RAIL

(2) 1X4

1X6
VERTICALS

(2) 1X4

7'-0"

3'-0"

SECTION
AT RAILING

1" BRASS
PIPE DOWELS
TYPICAL @
EACH POST

4" CONC. SLAB
ON GRAVEL BED.

7"

CARRY FND

BELOW LOCAL
FROST LINE

8" CONC. FND.

·MATERIAL LIST·

6	4"x4"/7' POSTS	
12	2"x6"/5' PLATES (CUT TO FIT)	
12	2"x6"/7' RAFTERS (" ")	
20	1"x6"/2'-6" RAIL VERTICALS	
20	1"x4"/5' RAIL TOP & BOTTOM	
5	5/4"x6"/5' HANDRAIL	
135	LIN. FT. 1" LATTICE	

6   1"∅ x 8" BRASS DOWELS
1   3/8"x6'x6' PLYWOOD SOFFIT
6   1"x4" CORNICE BOARD
126 SQ. FT. ROOF AREA FOR 3/8" PLYWOOD
      SHEATHING AND ROOF SHINGLES.
21   CU. FT. OF CONC. FOUNDATION FOR
      1'-0" OF DEPTH (MULTIPLY 21 X EA.
      FT. OF REQ. DEPTH).

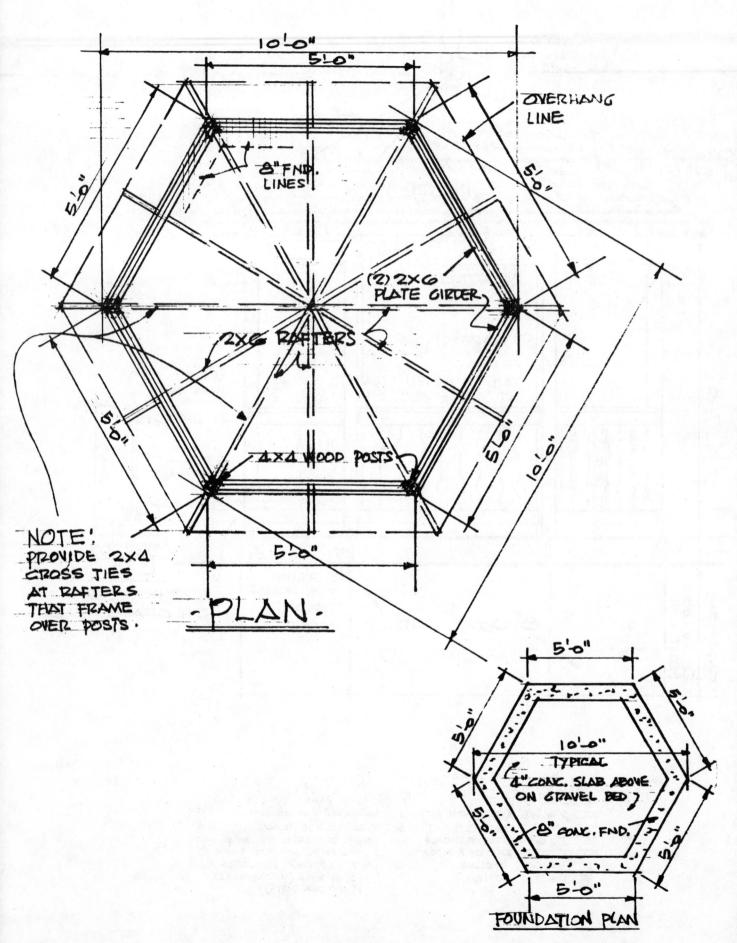

OVERHANG LINE

8" FND. LINES

(2) 2X6 PLATE GIRDER

2X6 RAFTERS

4X4 WOOD POSTS

10'-0"
5'-0"
5'-0"
5'-0"
5'-0"
5'-0"
5'-0"
5'-0"
10'-0"

NOTE!
PROVIDE 2X4 CROSS TIES AT RAFTERS THAT FRAME OVER POSTS.

-PLAN-

FOUNDATION PLAN

5'-0"
5'-0"
5'-0"
5'-0"
10'-0"
5'-0"
5'-0"
5'-0"

TYPICAL

4" CONC. SLAB ABOVE ON GRAVEL BED

8" CONC. FND.

13.

TEPEE GAZEBO

Six-sided open garden room

A yard is a yard is a yard, but it can be much more. It can, if you plan it that way, be the place where you spend most of your summer time. Make your yard inviting. A gazebo, such as the tepee-inspired design that's pictured here, is sure to lure you outdoors more often. It has a slatted roof that allows for filtered shade. Picnic table can be placed inside for outdoor eating. Screen in sides and roof, if you like. Gazebo is 10 by 10 feet; 17 feet high.

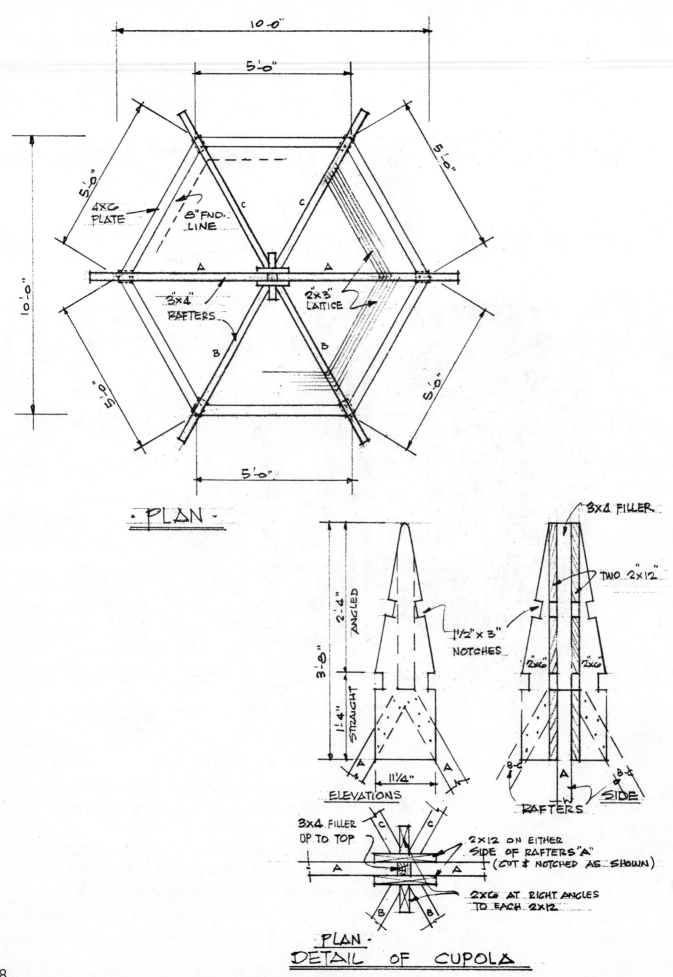

10'-0"

5'-0"

5'-0"

5'-0"

5'-0"

5'-0"

5'-0"

4X6 PLATE

8" FND. LINE

C   C

A   A

3"x4" RAFTERS

2"x3" LATTICE

B   B

· PLAN ·

ELEVATIONS

3'-0"

2'-4" ANGLED

1'-4" STRAIGHT

11¼"

A   A

1½"x3" NOTCHES

3x4 FILLER

TWO 2x12

2"x6"   2"x6"

B-C   B-C

A

RAFTERS   SIDE

W

3x4 FILLER UP TO TOP

C   C

A   A

B   B

2x12 ON EITHER SIDE OF RAFTERS "A" (CUT & NOTCHED AS SHOWN)

2x6 AT RIGHT ANGLES TO EACH 2x12

· PLAN ·

DETAIL OF CUPOLA

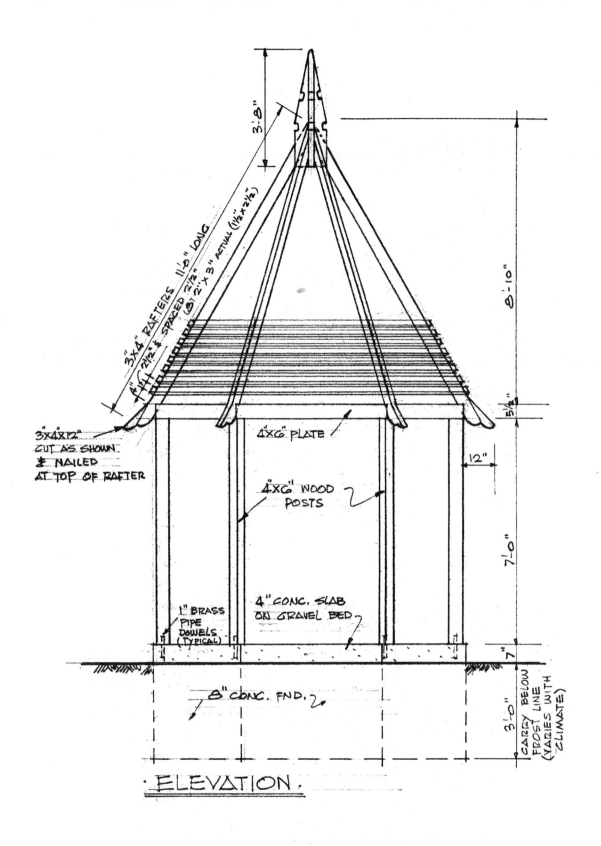

3"x4" RAFTERS 11'0" LONG

2"x 3" ACTUAL (1½"x 2½")

SPACED 2½" &
(8")

4"x 2½" &

3"x4"x12"
CUT AS SHOWN
& NAILED
AT TOP OF RAFTER

4"x6" PLATE

4"x6" WOOD
POSTS

1" BRASS
PIPE
DOWELS
(TYPICAL)

4" CONC. SLAB
ON GRAVEL BED

12"

8" CONC. FND.

3'-8"

8'-10"

5½"

7'-0"

7"

3'-0"

CARRY BELOW
FROST LINE
(VARIES WITH
CLIMATE)

·ELEVATION·

MATERIAL LIST

6	4"x6"/7'-0"	POSTS
6	4"x6"/5'-0"	PLATES CUT TO FIT
6	3"x4"/11'-0"	RAFTERS " "
1	3"x4"/6'-0"	RAFTER ENDS
240	LIN. FT 2"x3"	ROOF LATTICE
1	3"x4"/3'	FILLER AT TOP
2	2"x6"/3'-8"	TOP
2	2"x12"/3'-8"	TOP

PASSIVE SOLAR SPACES

(used by active people and plants)

14

SOLARIUM TEA ROOM

Saves money on fuel

Add a solarium: The newest status symbol for home owners is a solarium. It can be as compact as this 12'4'' by 8' room or larger. In winter, the solarium gathers solar energy that can be blown into the main house to lower heating bills; in summer, exhaust fans at both ends blow out hot air. Construction is redwood with corrugated plastic roof. The room is large enough for a table if your family enjoys dining with a garden view—and in this room, winter as well as summer, there is one.

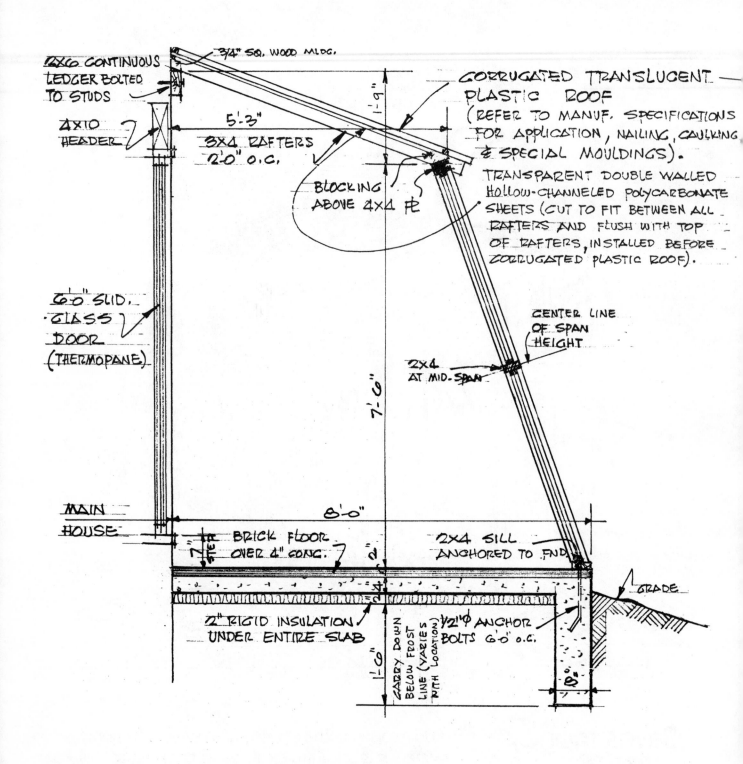

3/4" SQ. WOOD MLDG.

2X6 CONTINUOUS LEDGER BOLTED TO STUDS

CORRUGATED TRANSLUCENT PLASTIC ROOF (REFER TO MANUF. SPECIFICATIONS FOR APPLICATION, NAILING, CAULKING & SPECIAL MOULDINGS).

4X10 HEADER

5'-3"

3X4 RAFTERS 2'-0" O.C.

1'-9"

BLOCKING ABOVE 4X4 ℞

TRANSPARENT DOUBLE WALLED HOLLOW-CHANNELED POLYCARBONATE SHEETS (CUT TO FIT BETWEEN ALL RAFTERS AND FLUSH WITH TOP OF RAFTERS, INSTALLED BEFORE CORRUGATED PLASTIC ROOF).

CENTER LINE OF SPAN HEIGHT

6'-0" SLID. GLASS DOOR (THERMOPANE)

7'-6"

2X4 AT MID-SPAN

MAIN HOUSE

8'-0"

BRICK FLOOR OVER 4" CONC.

2X4 SILL ANCHORED TO FND.

GRADE

2" RIGID INSULATION UNDER ENTIRE SLAB

CARRY DOWN BELOW FROST LINE (VARIES WITH LOCATION)

1/2"⌀ ANCHOR BOLTS 6'-0" O.C.

1'-0"

· MATERIAL LIST ·

9	2X4	8'-0" LONG
2	4X4	8'-0" LONG
7	2X4	6'-0" LONG
	4X4	(1) 12'-4", (1) 10'-0" ℞
	2X4	(1) 12'-4", + 32 LIN FT (SIDE ℞ & SILL)
235	SQ. FT.	POLYCARBONATE SHEETS
74	SQ. FT.	CORRUGATED PLASTIC (ROOF)
360	LIN. FT.	3/4"X 3/4" SQ. EDGE WOOD MOULDING
100	SQ. FT.	COMMON BRICK (FLOOR)
1		3/4" X 4'-0" X 5'-0" GROOVED PLYWOOD
1		6'-0" X 6'-8" SLID. GL. DOOR (THERMOPANE)

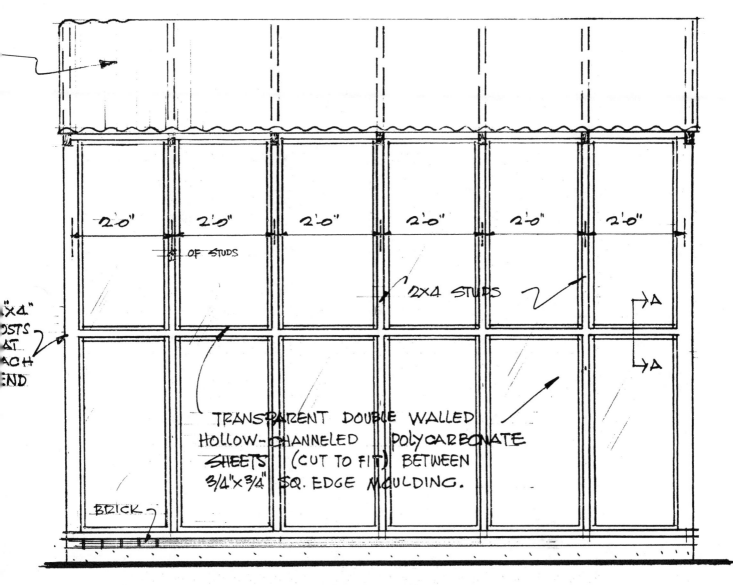

2'-0"   2'-0"   2'-0"   2'-0"   2'-0"   2'-0"

OF STUDS

2X4 STUDS

→A

→A

TRANSPARENT DOUBLE WALLED HOLLOW-CHANNELED POLYCARBONATE SHEETS (CUT TO FIT) BETWEEN 3/4"x3/4" SQ. EDGE MOULDING.

"X4" OSTS AT ACH END

BRICK

·ELEVATION·

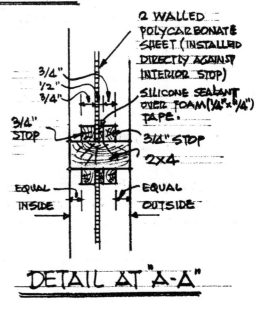

2 WALLED POLYCARBONATE SHEET (INSTALLED DIRECTLY AGAINST INTERIOR STOP)

3/4"
1/2"
3/4"

3/4" STOP

SILICONE SEALANT OVER FOAM (1/4"x1/4") TAPE.

3/4" STOP
2X4

EQUAL INSIDE

EQUAL OUTSIDE

DETAIL AT "A-A"

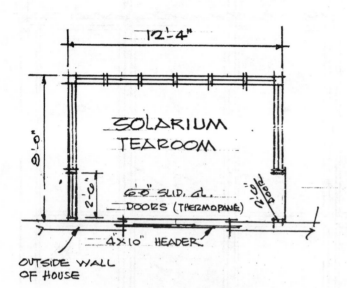

SOLARIUM
TEAROOM

12'-4"

8'-0"

2'-0"

6'-0" SLID. GL.
DOORS (THERMOPANE)

2'-0" DOOR

4'X10" HEADER

OUTSIDE WALL
OF HOUSE

FLOOR PLAN

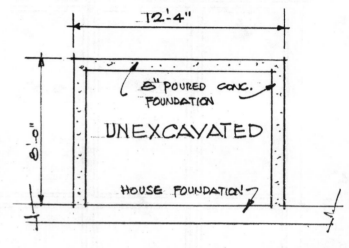

12'-4"

8'-0"

8" POURED CONC.
FOUNDATION

UNEXCAVATED

HOUSE FOUNDATION

FOUNDATION PLAN.

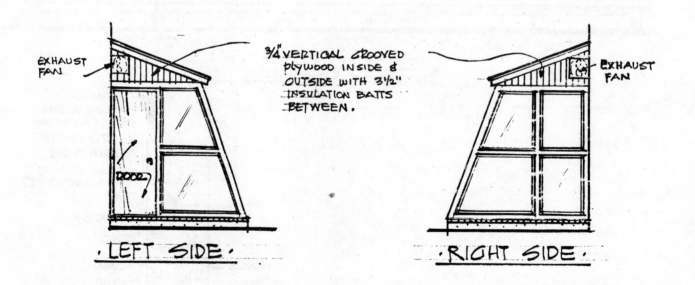

EXHAUST
FAN

DOOR

LEFT SIDE.

3/4" VERTICAL GROOVED
PLYWOOD INSIDE &
OUTSIDE WITH 3½"
INSULATION BATTS
BETWEEN.

EXHAUST
FAN

RIGHT SIDE

15.

BASEMENT SOLARIUM

Brighten a basement and warm it at the same time

Add a solarium: Brighten a basement room by adding a solarium 12 feet, 11 inches wide; 3 feet deep; room height. It can be added to an existing home or included in plans for a new one. Built on the south side of the house, it provides solar heat. Fluorescent lighting is concealed at top. The finish is stone facing.

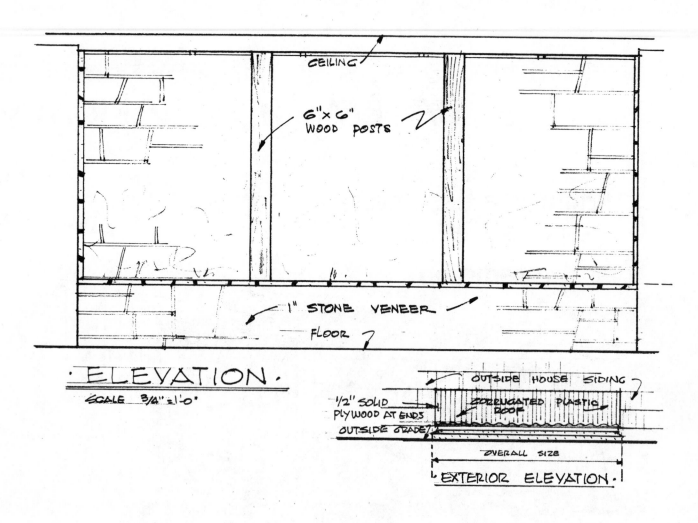

CEILING

6"x 6" WOOD POSTS

1" STONE VENEER

FLOOR

· ELEVATION ·
SCALE 3/4"=1'-0"

OUTSIDE HOUSE SIDING

1/2" SOLID
PLYWOOD AT ENDS

CORRUGATED PLASTIC
ROOF

OUTSIDE GRADE

OVERALL SIZE

EXTERIOR ELEVATION.

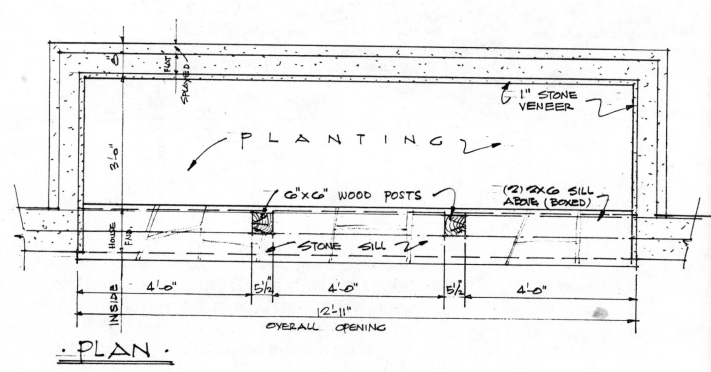

FLAT

SPLAYED

1" STONE VENEER

PLANTING

3'-0"

6"x6" WOOD POSTS

(2) 2x6 SILL
ABOVE (BOXED)

HOUSE FACE

STONE SILL

INSIDE FACE

4'-0"   5½"   4'-0"   5½"   4'-0"

12'-11"
OVERALL OPENING

· PLAN ·

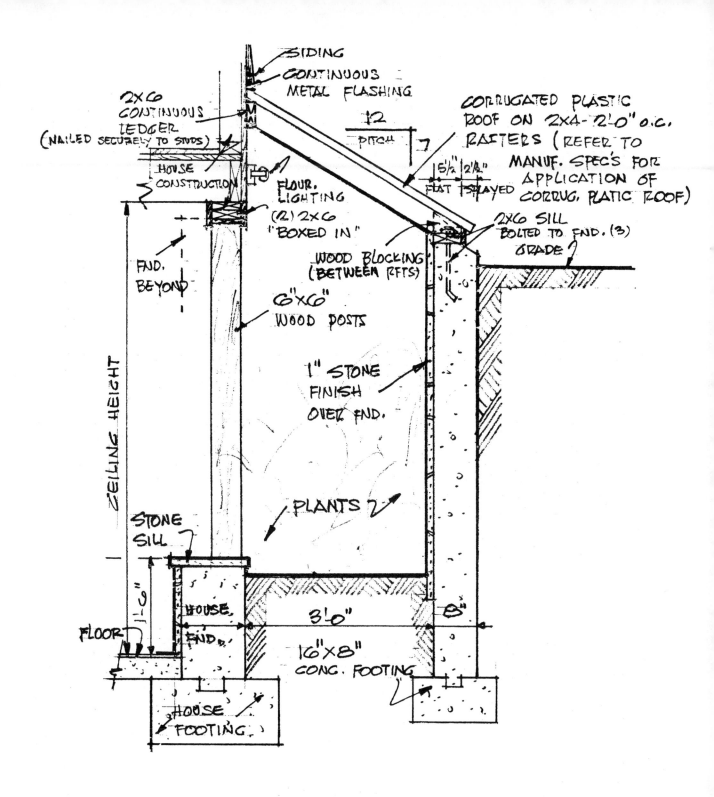

SIDING

CONTINUOUS
METAL FLASHING

CORRUGATED PLASTIC
ROOF ON 2x4-2'-0" o.c.
RAFTERS (REFER TO
MANUF. SPEC'S FOR
APPLICATION OF
CORRUG. PLATIC ROOF)

2x6
CONTINUOUS
LEDGER
(NAILED SECURELY TO STUDS)

HOUSE
CONSTRUCTION

12
PITCH 7

5½" 2'4"
FLAT SLAYED

2x6 SILL
BOLTED TO FND. (3)

GRADE

FLOUR.
LIGHTING
(2) 2x6
"BOXED IN"

WOOD BLOCKING
(BETWEEN RFTS)

FND.
BEYOND

6"x6"
WOOD POSTS

1" STONE
FINISH
OVER FND.

CEILING HEIGHT

PLANTS

STONE
SILL

HOUSE
FND.

3'-0"

8"

FLOOR

1'-9"

16"x8"
CONG. FOOTING

HOUSE
FOOTING

MATERIAL LIST

6	2x4	4'-0" LONG
2	2x6	14'-0" LONG
2	2x6	3'-0" LONG
56	SQ.FT.	CORRUGATED PLASTIC (ROOF)
2	6x6	5'-6" LONG (CUT TO FIT) POSTS
3	1x6	14'-0" LONG (CUT- FOR (2) 2x6 SILL)
100	SQ.FT.	1" STONE VENEER
131	SQ.FT.	CONCRETE
3		½"⌀ X10" ANCHOR RODS
1	8'-0"	FLOUR. LIGHTING FIXTURE

CHILDREN'S ACTIVITY HOUSES

(with storage for bikes, etcetera)

BUILD A CABOOSE

For children and storage

Don't hitch up this colorful caboose, build it in your yard and use one of its rooms for storage, the other for a playhouse or poolside dressing room. Built on a concrete block foundation, it has doors at either end, windows on both side walls. Waterproof canvas is stretched over the curved wood roof to form a finish. Vertical grooved siding can be painted in bright colors or stained, as you prefer; caboose is 6 feet, 3 inches wide by 14 feet, 8 inches long, including platforms at either end, by 8 feet, 7 inches high.

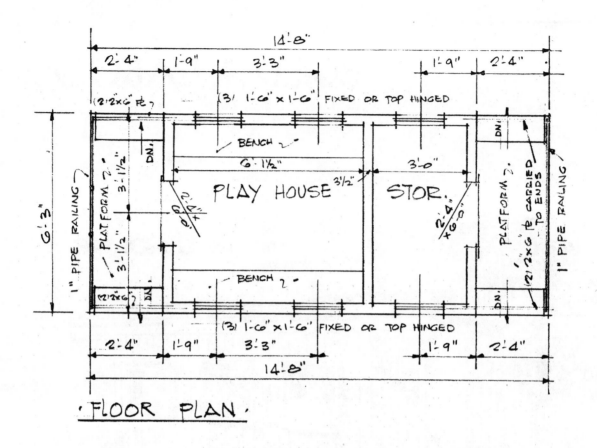

14'-8"

2'-4"   1'-9"   3'-3"   1'-9"   2'-4"

(2) 2x6 ft.

(3) 1'-6" x 1'-6" FIXED OR TOP HINGED

BENCH

6'-1½"

3'-1½"

PLATFORM

3'-1½"

6'-3"

1" PIPE RAILING

DN.

PLAY HOUSE 3½"

STOR.

3'-0"

2'-4" x 6'-0"

DN.

PLATFORM

(2) 2x6 ft CARRIED TO ENDS

1" PIPE RAILING

(2) 2x6 ft.

DN.

BENCH

(3) 1'-6" x 1'-6" FIXED OR TOP HINGED

2'-4"   1'-9"   3'-3"   1'-9"   2'-4"

14'-8"

· FLOOR PLAN ·

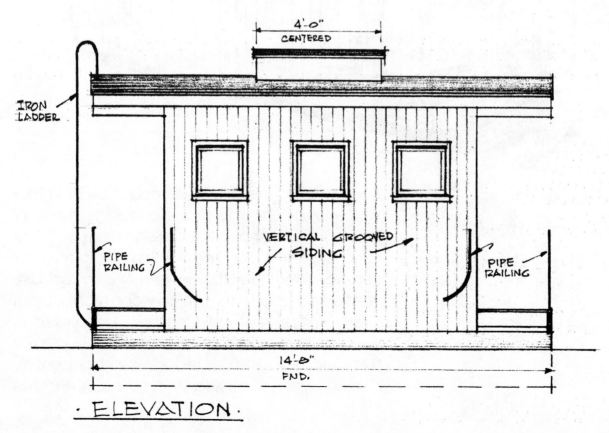

4'-0"

CENTERED

IRON LADDER

VERTICAL GROOVED SIDING

PIPE RAILING

PIPE RAILING

14'-8"

FND.

· ELEVATION ·

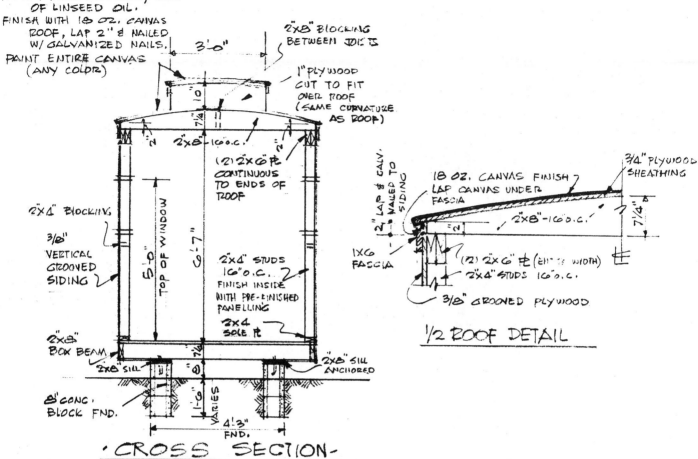

ROOF
- 2"×8"-16" O.C. CUT TO CURVE SHOWN (JOISTS)
- 3/4" EXTERIOR PLYWOOD SHEATHING
- PAINT PLYWOOD WITH HEAVY COAT OF LINSEED OIL.
- FINISH WITH 18 OZ. CANVAS ROOF, LAP 2" & NAILED W/ GALVANIZED NAILS, PAINT ENTIRE CANVAS (ANY COLOR)

2"×8" BLOCKING BETWEEN JOISTS

3'-0"

1" PLYWOOD CUT TO FIT OVER ROOF (SAME CURVATURE AS ROOF)

7 1/4"

2"×8"-16" O.C.

(2) 2"×6" ℄ CONTINUOUS TO ENDS OF ROOF

2"×4" BLOCKING

3/8" VERTICAL GROOVED SIDING

TOP OF WINDOW

5'-0"

9'-7"

2"×4" STUDS 16" O.C. FINISH INSIDE WITH PRE-FINISHED PANELLING

2×4 SOLE ℄

2"×8" BOX BEAM

2"×8" SILL

7 1/4"

2"×8" SILL ANCHORED

8" CONC. BLOCK FND.

1'-9"

VARIES

4'-3" FND.

·CROSS SECTION·

18 OZ. CANVAS FINISH
LAP CANVAS UNDER FASCIA

2" LAP & CALV. NAILED TO SIDING

3/4" PLYWOOD SHEATHING

2"×8"-16" O.C.

7 1/4"

1×6 FASCIA

(2) 2"×6" ℄ (ENTIRE WIDTH)

2"×4" STUDS 16" O.C.

3/8" GROOVED PLYWOOD

1/2 ROOF DETAIL

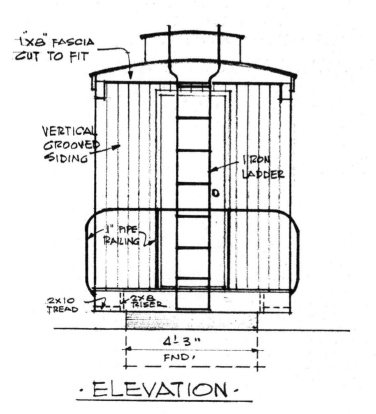

1×8 FASCIA CUT TO FIT

VERTICAL GROOVED SIDING

IRON LADDER

1" PIPE RAILING

2×10 TREAD

2×8 RISER

4'-3" FND.

· ELEVATION ·

MATERIAL LIST

LOCATION	SIZE	PIECES	LIN. FT.
FLOOR JOISTS	2×6	13/6'	78
ROOF JOISTS	2×8	11/6'-3"	70
BOX BEAM	2×6	2/15'	30
BRIDGING @ ROOF	2×8	1/10'	10
PLATE ℄	2×6	4/15'	60
STUDS	2×4	40/6'	240
SOLE ℄ & BLOCKING	2×4	—	76
TREAD	2×10	1/10	10
FLOORING	3/4" PLY.	91	SQ. FT.
ROOF SHEATHING	3/8"PLY	91	SQ. FT.
SIDE WALLS	3/8"	187	SQ. FT.
CONC. BLOCK	8"×16"	84 UNITS	
WINDOWS	1'-6" SQ.	6 UNITS	
DOORS	2'×6'	2 UNITS	

61

17.

PLAY TRAIN FOR THE YARD

All aboard
for fun

Make your yard the talk of the town by building this playtime locomotive. In the cab, there are built-in benches and the entrance to a tunnel that leads out front. Construction is wood on concrete block foundation.

The locomotive is 12 feet long; 4 feet wide at front, 6 feet wide for rear cab; height is 6 feet, 4 inches.

Paint the play train bright colors and your youngsters will love it. So will every kid in the neighborhood.

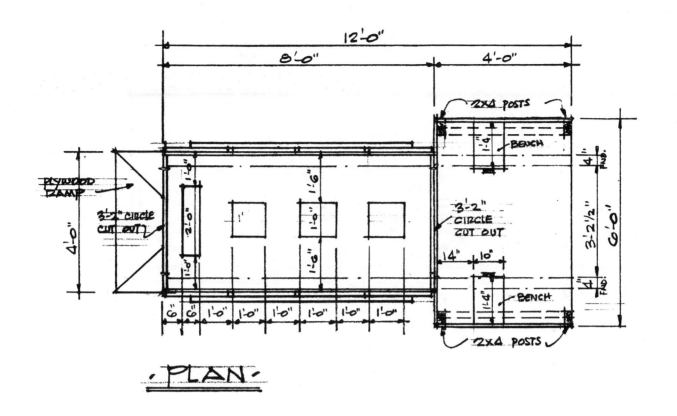

12'-0"
8'-0"
4'-0"

2x4 POSTS

BENCH

PLYWOOD RAMP

3'-2" CIRCLE CUT OUT

3'-2" CIRCLE CUT OUT

4'-0"

1'-6"

1'-0"

2'-0"

14" 10"

BENCH

3'-2½"

6'-0"

2x4 POSTS

6" 6" 1'-0" 1'-0" 1'-0" 1'-0" 1'-0" 1'-0"

· PLAN ·

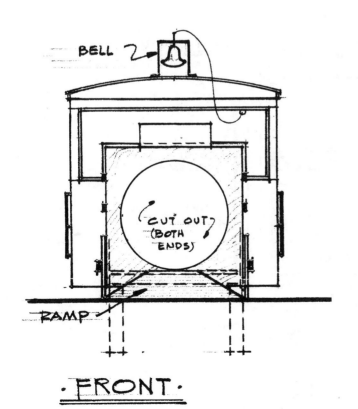

BELL

CUT OUT (BOTH ENDS)

RAMP

· FRONT ·

MATERIAL LIST

LOCATION	SIZE	PIECES	
FLOOR JOISTS	2x4	7/4'	4/6'
ROOF JOISTS	2x8	4/6'	
BOX BEAM	2x4	3/8'	
POSTS	2x4	4/6'	
PLATES (TOP)	2x4	4/4'	
BOTTOM PL	2x4	2/4'	
FLOORING	3/4" PLY.	1-4'x8'	1-4'x6'
ROOF SHEATHING	1/2" PLY.	1-4'x8'	
WALLS & TOP (FRONT)	3/8" PLY.	4-4'x8'	
WALLS (REAR)	3/4" PLY	3-4'x6	
WINDOW FRAME	1'x2'	50 LIN. FT.	
WHEELS	3/4" PLY	1-4'x8	
MISC.	2'x4"	4/6'	2/7
BENCH	1'x10"	1/3'	

63

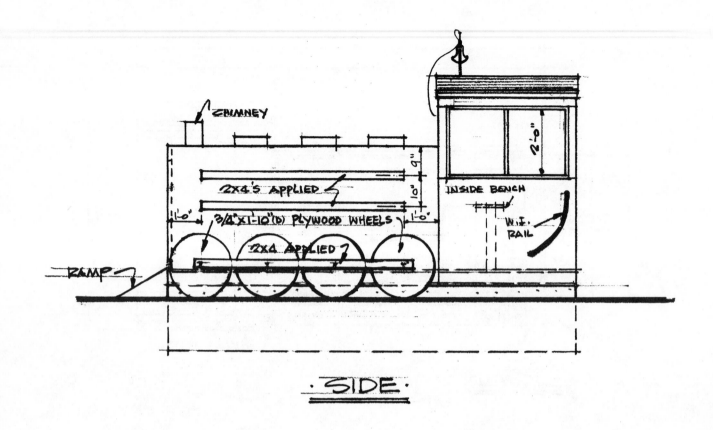

CHIMNEY

2x4'S APPLIED

3/4"x1-10"(D) PLYWOOD WHEELS

2x4 APPLIED

RAMP

9"

10"

1'0"

1'0"

INSIDE BENCH

2'0"

W.I. RAIL

· SIDE ·

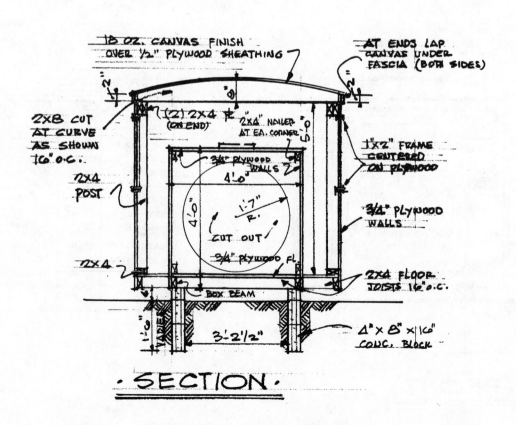

18 OZ. CANVAS FINISH OVER 1/2" PLYWOOD SHEATHING

AT ENDS LAP CANVAS UNDER FASCIA (BOTH SIDES)

2x8 CUT AT CURVE AS SHOWN 16" O.C.

(2) 2x4 (ON END)

2x4 NAILED AT EA. CORNER

1"x2" FRAME CENTERED ON PLYWOOD

2x4 POST

3/4" PLYWOOD WALLS

4'0"

3/4" PLYWOOD WALLS

4'0"

1'-7" R'

CUT OUT

3/4" PLYWOOD FL.

2x4

2x4 FLOOR JOISTS 16" O.C.

BOX BEAM

VARIES

1'0"

3'-2 1/2"

4"x 8" x 16" CONC. BLOCK

· SECTION ·

18

A-FRAME PLAYHOUSE

It's easy to build

Playhouse plan: Instead of pitching a tent, the kids will enjoy having their own A-frame playhouse. It's easy to build with 4' x 8' plywood used for each side of roof. Wood deck projects forward to form a front porch. Fence is a nice finishing touch. Ideal for summer sleep-outs, playhouse is 7 feet wide by 8 feet high with a 6-foot, 3-inch deep deck.

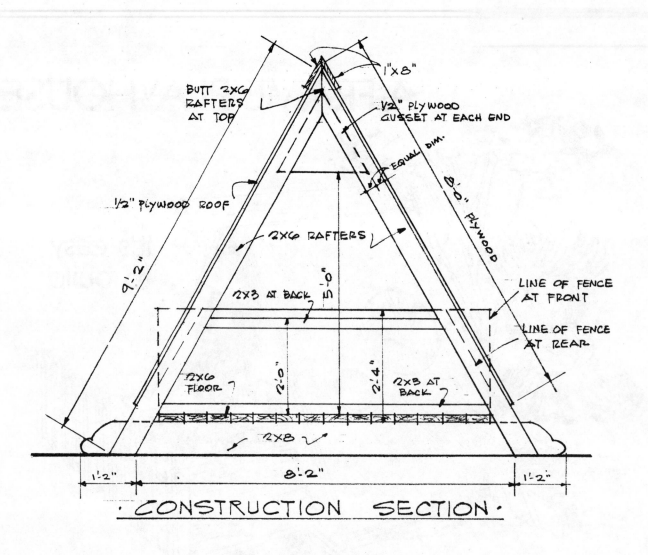

BUTT 2×6
RAFTERS
AT TOP

1"×8"

1/2" PLYWOOD
GUSSET AT EACH END

EQUAL DIM.

8'-0" PLYWOOD

1/2" PLYWOOD ROOF

9'-2"

2×6 RAFTERS

2×3 AT BACK

5'-0"

LINE OF FENCE
AT FRONT

LINE OF FENCE
AT REAR

2×6
FLOOR

2'-0"

2'-4"

2×3 AT
BACK

2×8

1'-2"

8'-2"

1'-2"

· CONSTRUCTION SECTION ·

MATERIAL LIST

4	2×6 RAFTERS 9'-2" LONG
2	2×8 FLOOR JOISTS 10'-6" LONG
14	2×6 FLOORING 6'-3" LONG
30	LIN. FT. 2×3" RAIL FRAME
28	LIN. FT. 1"×4" FRONT RAILING
2	1/2"×4'×8' PLYWOOD ROOF
1	1/2"×4'×7' PLYWOOD BACK RAIL
	& GUSSETS
2	1"×8"×5'-0" TOP RIDGE COVER

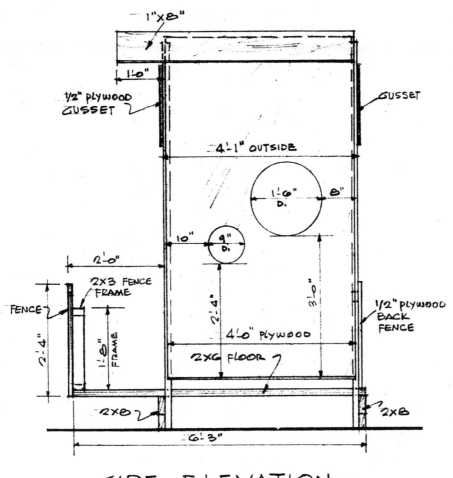

1"X8"

1'0"

1/2" PLYWOOD
GUSSET

GUSSET

4'-1" OUTSIDE

1'-6"
D.

8"

10"

9"
D.

3'-0"

2'-0"

2X3 FENCE
FRAME

FENCE

2'-4"

1'-6"
FRAME

2'-4"

1/2" PLYWOOD
BACK
FENCE

4'-0" PLYWOOD

2X6 FLOOR

2X8

2X8

6'-3"

· SIDE ELEVATION ·

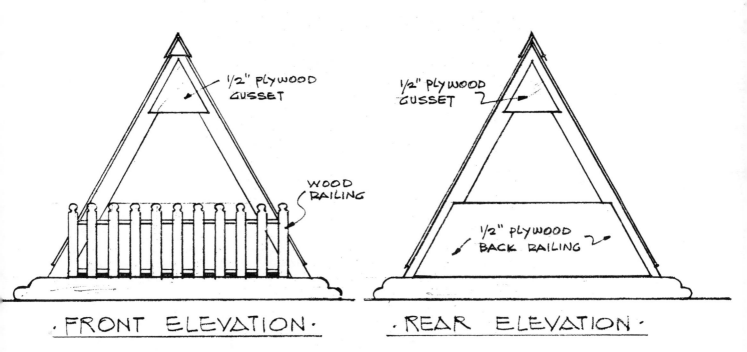

1/2" PLYWOOD
GUSSET

WOOD
RAILING

1/2" PLYWOOD
GUSSET

1/2" PLYWOOD
BACK RAILING

· FRONT ELEVATION ·

· REAR ELEVATION ·

BARNS FOR
PEOPLE AND CARS

(or boats and goats)

19

GAMBREL ROOFED "BARN"

There's a spiral stairway in the silo

Lofty garage: The two-car garage grows in prestige with the addition of a loft that can be a studio or made into an apartment. Silo houses stairs that lead to the loft and gives the structure a farm look. The loft is dividable into four rooms, each with a window and suitable for an office. The garage-loft is 21 feet high, 24 feet, 4 inches wide and 23 feet deep. Exterior is painted with personal choice of colors.

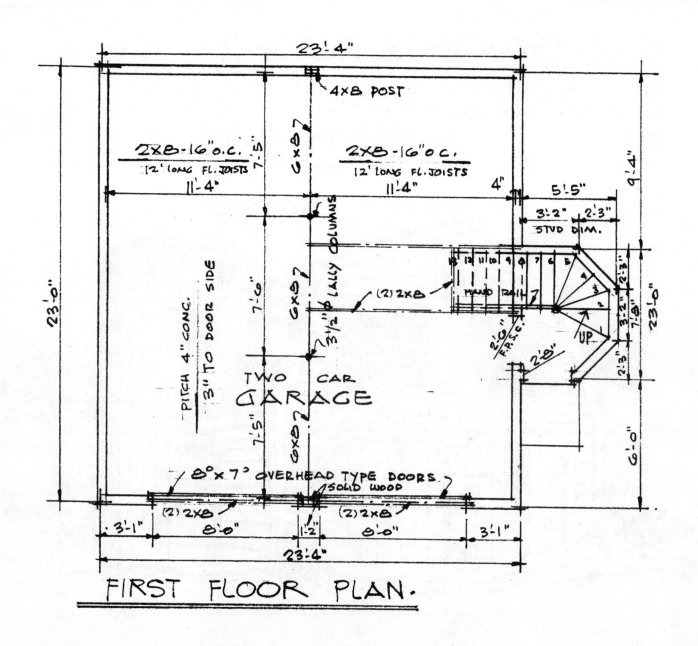

FIRST FLOOR PLAN.

FRAMING LUMBER LIST ('=FEET)					SILO RFTS' & TIES	2x4	—	64'
location	SIZE	amount	lin.ft.		CEIL. JOISTS	2x8	18/19'	342'
STUDS	2x4	134/8, 28/12, 15/9'	1383'		FLOOR JOISTS	2x8	36/12'	432'
PLATES & SILL	2x4	—	422'		PURLIN	2x8	2/23'	46'
GARAGE RAFTERS	2x6	36/10', 32/9'	648'		RIDGE	2x8	1/29' INCL. BLOCK	29'

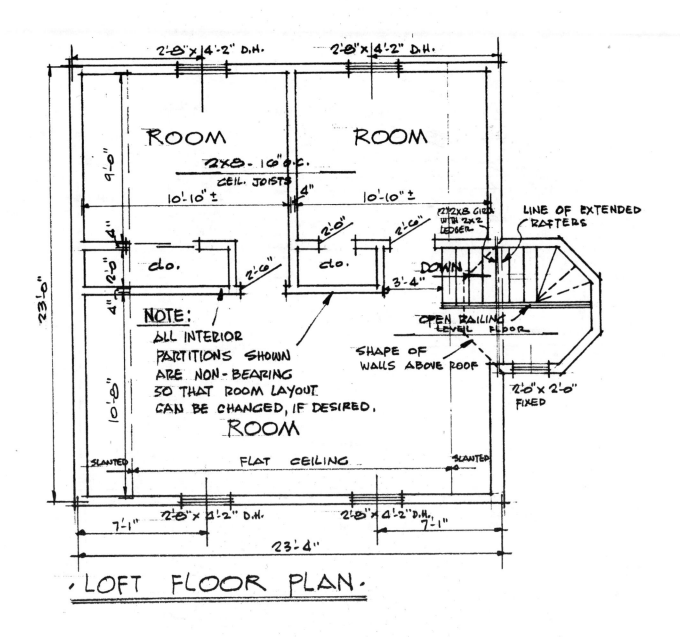

.LOFT FLOOR PLAN.

ROOM   **ROOM**

2×8 - 16" o.c.
CEIL. JOISTS

10'-10" ±   4"   10'-10" ±

2'-0"x 4'-2" D.H.   2'-0"x 4'-2" D.H.

9'-0"
4"
2'-0"
4"
23'-0"
10'-0"

clo.   2'-0"   clo.   2'-0"

3'-4"

(2) 2×8 GIRDER
WITH 2×2
LEDGER

DOWN

OPEN RAILING
LEVEL FLOOR

SHAPE OF
WALLS ABOVE ROOF

LINE OF EXTENDED
RAFTERS

2'-0"x 2'-0"
FIXED

NOTE:
ALL INTERIOR
PARTITIONS SHOWN
ARE NON-BEARING
SO THAT ROOM LAYOUT
CAN BE CHANGED, IF DESIRED.

ROOM

FLAT CEILING

SLANTED   SLANTED

7'-1"   2'-0"x 4'-2" D.H.   2'-0"x 4'-2" D.H.   7'-1"

23'-4"

COLLAR BMS.	2×4	18/8'	144'
GIRDER	6×8	1/23'	23'
DOOR HEADER	4×8	4/9'	36'
SHEATHING	LOFT SUB. FL.	5/8" PLYWOOD	514 sq. ft.
	SIDE WALLS	3/8" "	833 " "
	ROOF	1/2" "	938 " "

71

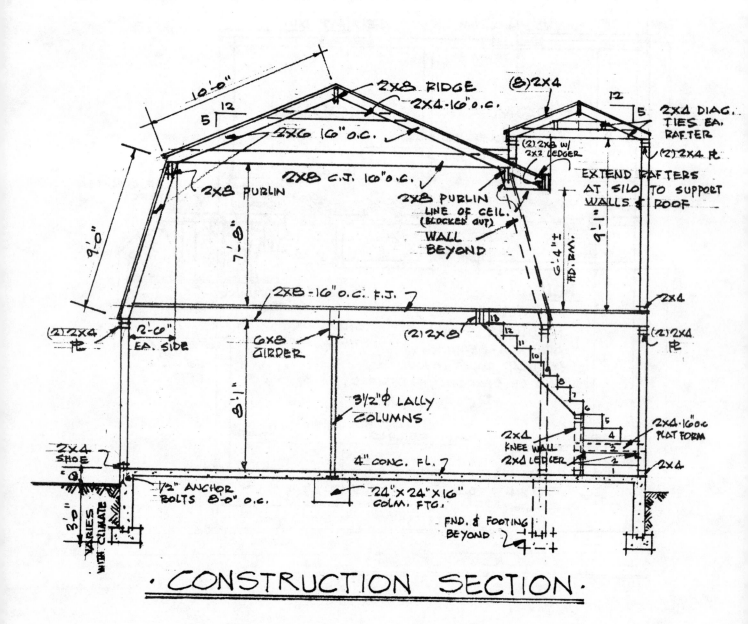

· CONSTRUCTION SECTION ·

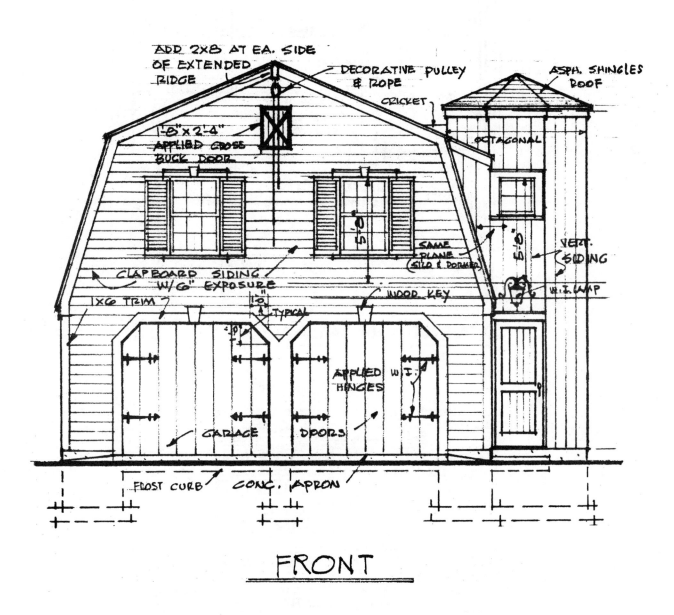

ADD 2X8 AT EA. SIDE
OF EXTENDED
RIDGE

DECORATIVE PULLEY
& ROPE

CRICKET

ASPH. SHINGLES
ROOF

1'-8" X 2'-4"
APPLIED CROSS
BUCK DOOR

OCTAGONAL

SAME
PLANE
(SILO & DORMER)

VERT.
SIDING

CLAPBOARD SIDING
W/6" EXPOSURE

1X6 TRIM

1'-0"
TYPICAL

WOOD KEY

W.I. LAMP

APPLIED W.I.
HINGES

GARAGE   DOORS

FROST CURB   CONC. APRON

FRONT

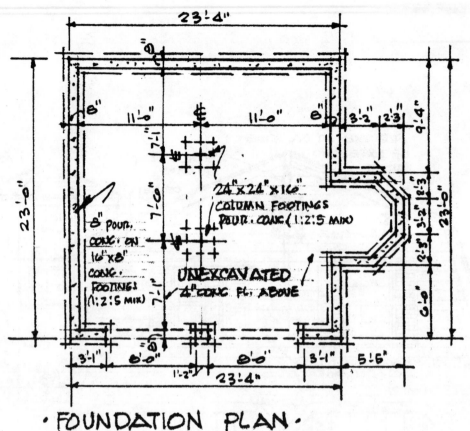

· FOUNDATION PLAN ·

Labels within plan:
- 23'-4"
- 8"
- 11'-0"
- 11'-0"
- 8"
- 3'-2"
- 2'-3"
- 9'-4"
- 7'-1"
- 7'-0"
- 23'-0"
- 24"x24"x16" COLUMN FOOTINGS POUR. CONC. (1:2:5 MIX)
- 8" POUR. CONC. ON 16"x8" CONC. FOOTINGS (1:2:5 MIX)
- UNEXCAVATED 4" CONC. FL. ABOVE
- 3'-2"
- 2'-3"
- 2'-3"
- 23'-0"
- 6'-0"
- 7'-1"
- 7'-1"
- 3'-1"
- 8'-0"
- 1'-2"
- 8'-0"
- 3'-1"
- 5'-6"
- 23'-4"

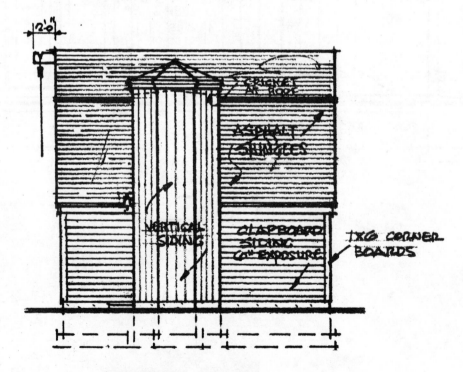

· RIGHT SIDE ELEVATION ·

Labels within elevation:
- 12'-0"
- CRICKET AT ROOF
- ASPHALT SHINGLES
- VERTICAL SIDING
- CLAPBOARD SIDING 6" EXPOSURE
- 1x6 CORNER BOARDS

20

OLD DUTCH CLAPBOARD ONE-CAR GARAGE

With a two-story expansion apartment

If your year-round or vacation home lacks a garage, this one-car plan provides parking space plus a loft that has possibilities. You can use it for storage or utilize it as a hobby area, recreation room or guest quarters. If zoning permits, you might convert it into a three-room apartment for elderly in-laws, young-marrieds, or for rental income that can help pay off your home improvement loan.

Garage is 21 feet, 8 inches wide; 23 feet deep; 21 feet, 6 inches high.

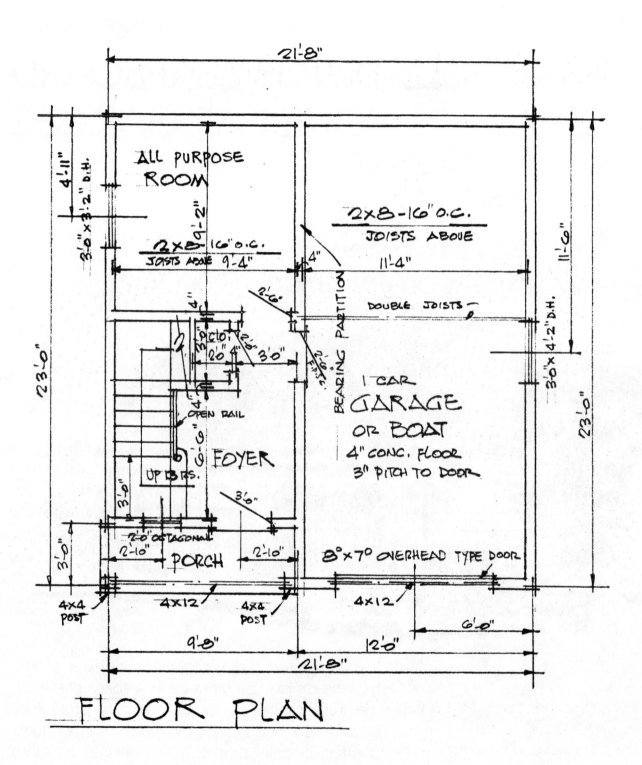

FLOOR PLAN

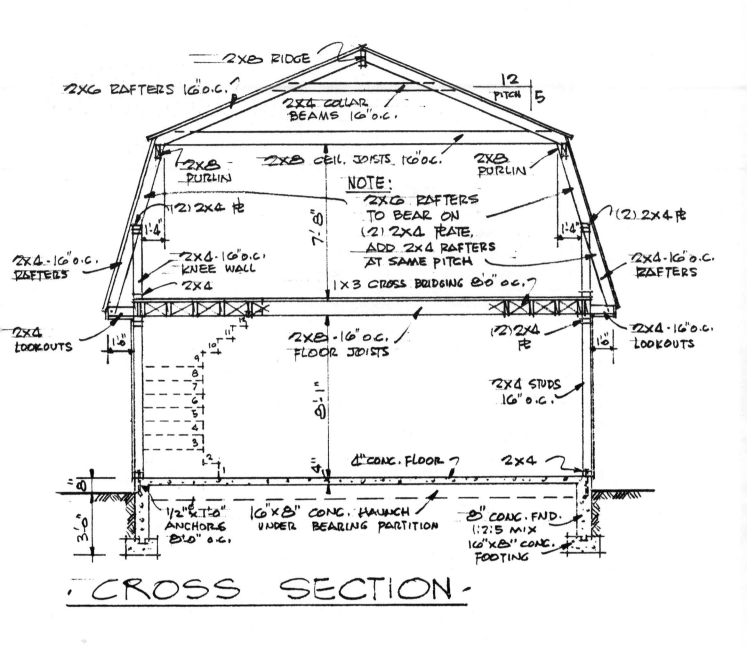

· CROSS SECTION ·

FRAMING LUMBER LIST			
LOCATION	SIZE	AMOUNT	LIN. FT.
STUDS	2×4	177/8' 52/4'	1624
PLATES & SILL	2×4	—	585
RAFTERS	2×6	36/12' 36/4'	676
CEIL. JOISTS	2×8	18/21	378
FL. JOISTS	2×8	18/12' 18/10'	396
PURLIN	2×8	2/23'	46

RIDGE	2×8	1/25'	25
COLLAR BEAMS	2×4	18/9'	162
HEADERS	4×12	2/9'	18
RAFTERS	2×4	36/5'	180
LOOKOUTS	2×4	36/1'	36

SHEATHING & FINISHING

LOFT SUB FLOOR, 5/8" PLYWOOD = 500☐'
SIDE WALLS , 3/8" PLYWOOD = 1028☐'
ROOF , 1/2" PLYWOOD = 948☐'

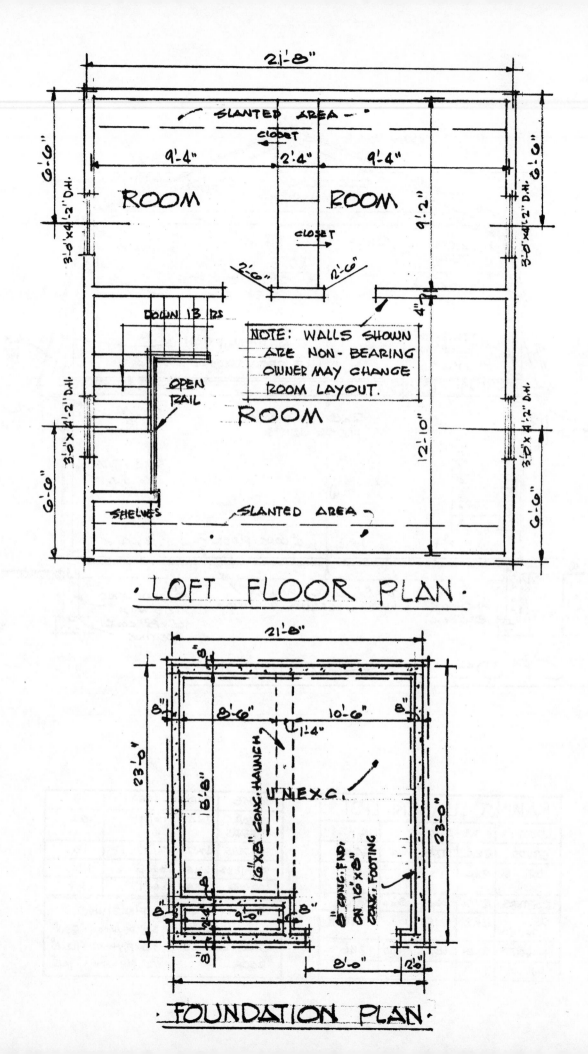

· LOFT FLOOR PLAN ·

· FOUNDATION PLAN ·

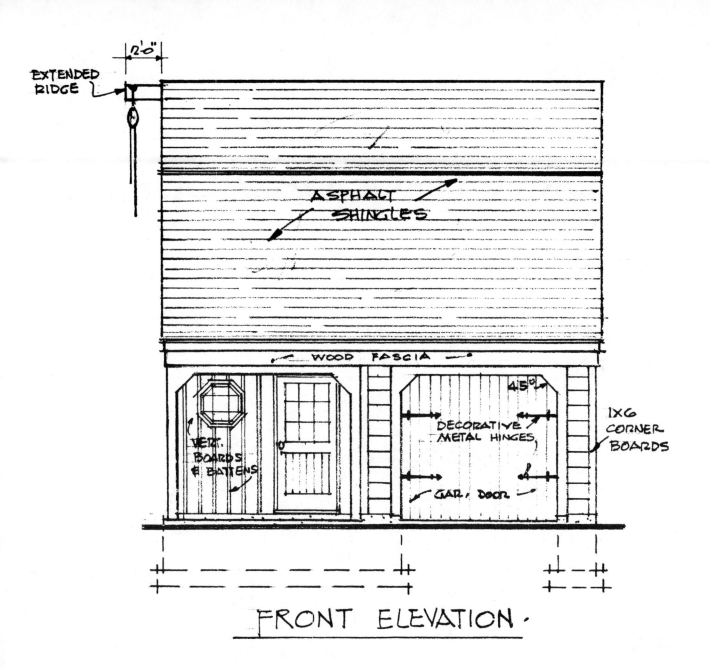

EXTENDED
RIDGE

2'-0"

ASPHALT
SHINGLES

WOOD FASCIA

VERT.
BOARDS
& BATTENS

DECORATIVE
METAL HINGES

45°

1X6
CORNER
BOARDS

GAR. DOOR

FRONT ELEVATION.

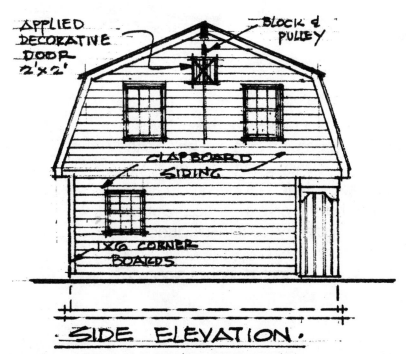

APPLIED
DECORATIVE
DOOR
2'X2'

BLOCK &
PULLEY

CLAPBOARD
SIDING

1X6 CORNER
BOARDS

SIDE ELEVATION.

21.

TUDOR COTTAGE GARAGE PLUS

Attic can be turned into an apartment

This plan provides a great deal more than a two-car garage because the expansion attic can be finished off to provide an efficiency apartment or, if you prefer, two (10 feet by 14 feet) rooms that can be utitlized for office, hobby or play space. Outside door leading to attic has entry foyer that includes access door to the garage. As shown, this chalet-style garage is 26 feet wide; 24 feet, 4 inches deep; 22 feet, 6 inches high.

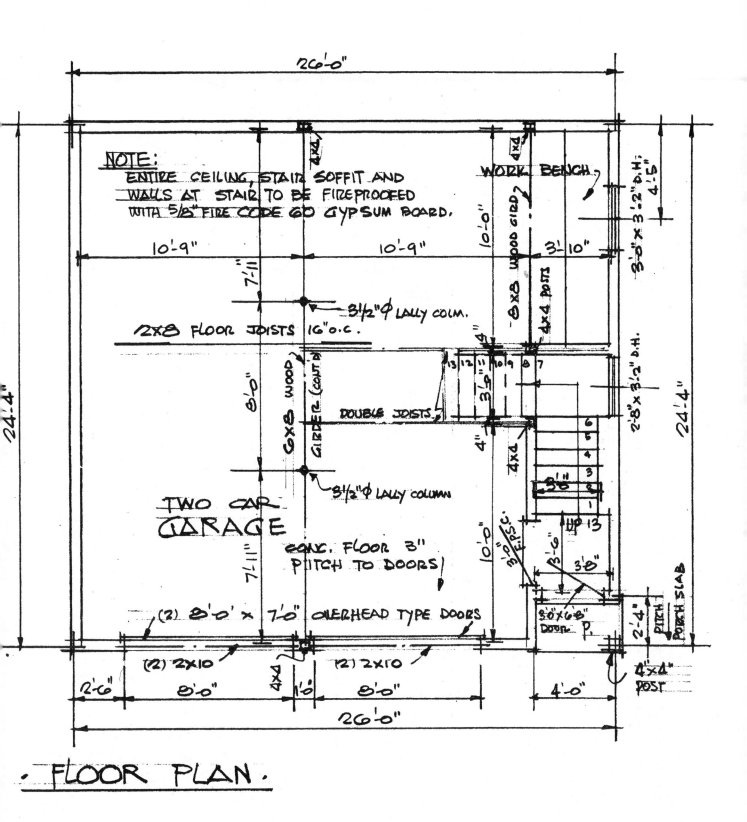

NOTE:
ENTIRE CEILING, STAIR SOFFIT AND
WALLS AT STAIR TO BE FIREPROOFED
WITH 5/8" FIRE CODE 60 GYPSUM BOARD.

26'-0"

10'-9"   10'-9"

WORK BENCH

4x4   4x4

10'-0"

3'-10"

3'-0" x 3'-2" D.H.

4'-5"

7'-11"

3½"∅ LALLY COLM.

12x8 FLOOR JOISTS 16" O.C.

8x8 WOOD GIRD.

4x4 POSTS

8'-0"

6x8 WOOD

GIRDER (CONT.)

DOUBLE JOISTS

13 12 11 10 9 8 7

3'-9"

2'-8" x 3'-2" D.H.

24'-4"

4"

4x4

6
5
4
3
2
1

3½"∅ LALLY column

5'-6"

3'-11"

TWO CAR
GARAGE

7'-11"

CONC. FLOOR 3"
PITCH TO DOORS

10'-0"

3" F.P.S.C.

UP 13

3'-0"

3'-8"

PITCH

PORCH SLAB

24'-4"

(2) 8'-0' x 7'-0" OVERHEAD TYPE DOORS

3'0" x 6'8"
DOOR

2'-4"

(2) 2x10   (2) 2x10

4x4

4x4" POST

2'-6"   8'-0"   1'-0"   8'-0"   4'-0"

26'-0"

· FLOOR PLAN ·

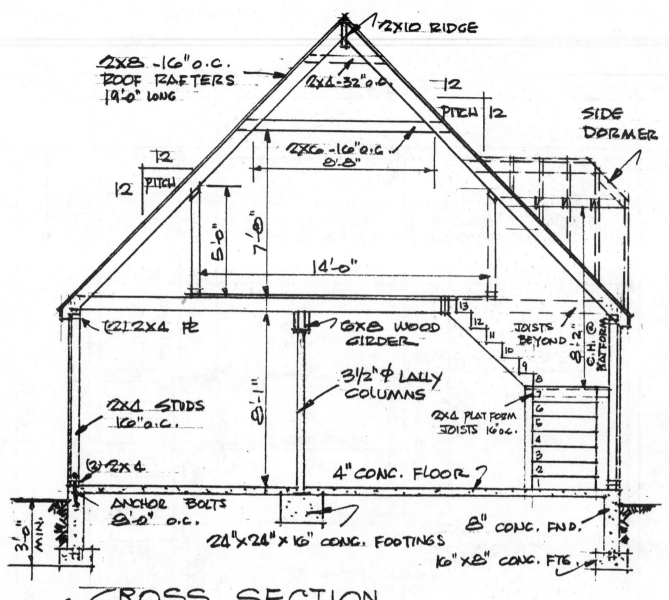

· CROSS SECTION ·

FRAMING LUMBER LIST			
LOCATION	SIZE	AMOUNT	LIN. FT.
STUDS	2×4	110/8', 37/5'	1065
PLATE & SILL	2×4	—	452
RAFTERS	2×8	40/19'	760
CEIL. TIES	2×6	19/10'	190
FLOOR JOISTS	2×8	19/22' 9/5'	463
RIDGE	2×10	1/25'	25
COLLAR BMS.	2×4	6/4'	24
GIRDER	6×10	1/25' & 1/11' (2×10)	25 & 11
DOOR HDR.	4×10	1/18	18

DORMER :			
RAFTERS	2×6	—	60
COLLAR TIES	2×4	5/4'	20
RIDGE	2×8	1/6'	6
POSTS	4×4	5/8'	40
VALLEY RAFTERS	4×10	2/24 2/12	72
SUB-FLOOR	3/4" PLY.	●364 SQ. FT	— (ATTIC)
WALL SHEATHING	1/2" PLY.	●972 SQ. FT	—
ROOF SHEATHING	1/2" PLY.	●950 SQ. FT	—

AMOUNTS SHOWN CAN
ALSO BE USED TO
COMPUTE FINISHING
MATERIALS REQUIRED

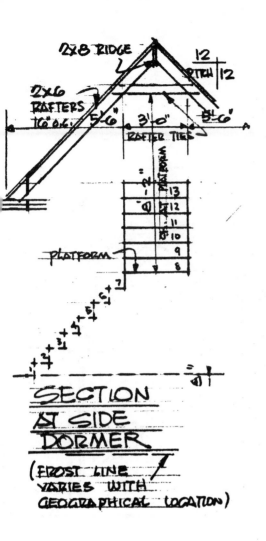

2×8 RIDGE

2×6 RAFTERS 16" O.C.

12 / PITCH / 12

5'-6"   3'-0"   5'-6"

RAFTER TIES

PLATFORM

13
12
11
10
9
8
7

PLATFORM

SECTION AT SIDE DORMER

(FROST LINE VARIES WITH GEOGRAPHICAL LOCATION)

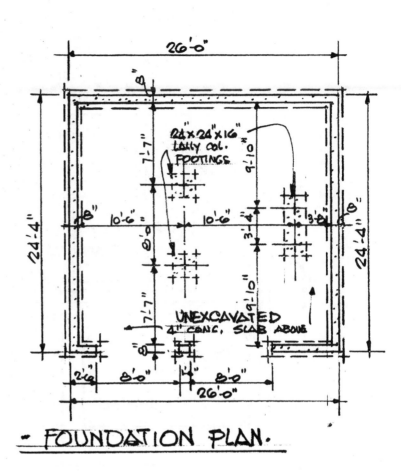

26'-0"

8"

24'-4"

24"×24"×16" LALLY COL. FOOTINGS

7'-7"   8'   9'-10"

8"   10'-6"   10'-6"   3'-4"   3'-0"

8'-0"

7'-7"   9'-10"

UNEXCAVATED
4" CONC. SLAB ABOVE

2'-6"   8'-0"   4"   8'-0"

26'-0"

· FOUNDATION PLAN ·

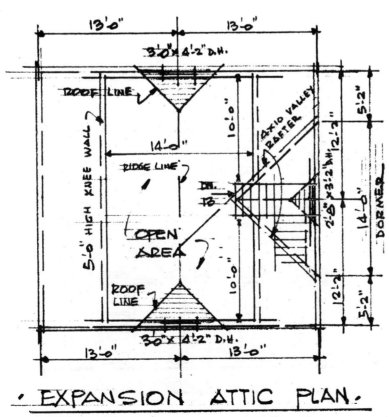

13'-0"   13'-0"

3'-0" × 4'-2" D.H.

ROOF LINE

5'-0" HIGH KNEE WALL

10'-0"

14'-0"

RIDGE LINE

DN. 13

OPEN AREA

10'-0"

ROOF LINE

4×10 VALLEY RAFTER

5'-2"   12'-2"   2'-6"×3'-2" D.H.

14'-0" DORMER

12'-2"   5'-2"

30" × 4'-2" D.H.

13'-0"   13'-0"

· EXPANSION ATTIC PLAN ·

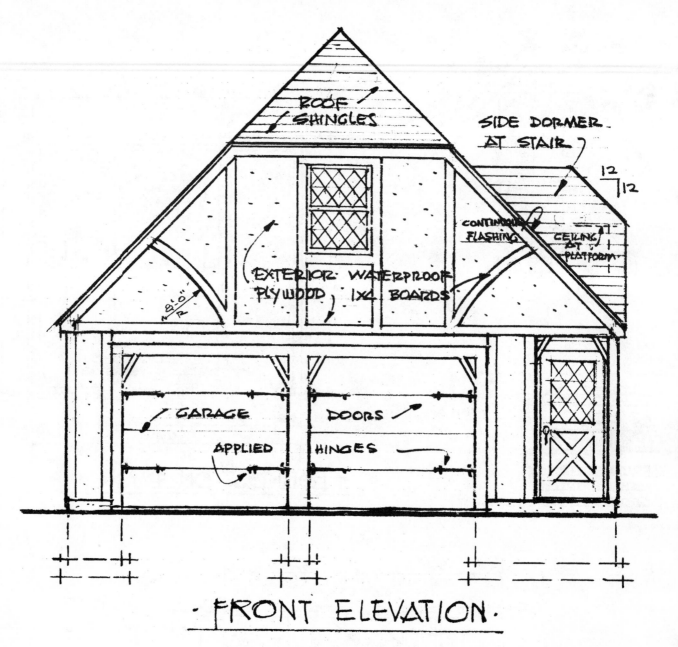

ROOF SHINGLES

SIDE DORMER. AT STAIR

EXTERIOR WATERPROOF PLYWOOD 1X4 BOARDS

CONTINUOUS FLASHING

CEILING AT PLATFORM

9'-0" R

GARAGE DOORS

APPLIED HINGES

12/12

FRONT ELEVATION.

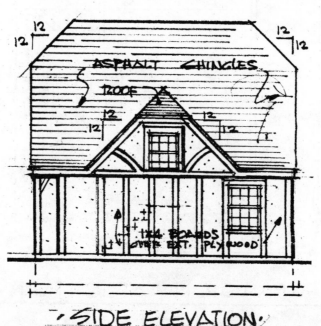

ASPHALT SHINGLES

ROOF

1X4 BOARDS OVER EXT. PLYWOOD

12/12

12/12

12/12

12/12

SIDE ELEVATION.

22

MEDITERRANEAN STUCCO GARAGE

600 sq. ft. apartment upstairs

This two-car garage has a bonus of space that can be converted into an apartment or an office for a professional. Upper floor is large enough for kitchen, bath, living room, two bedrooms. Garage area includes an alcove for workbench. Entry (left) has access to apartment and garage. Garage is 26 feet wide; 23 feet deep, 21 feet high.

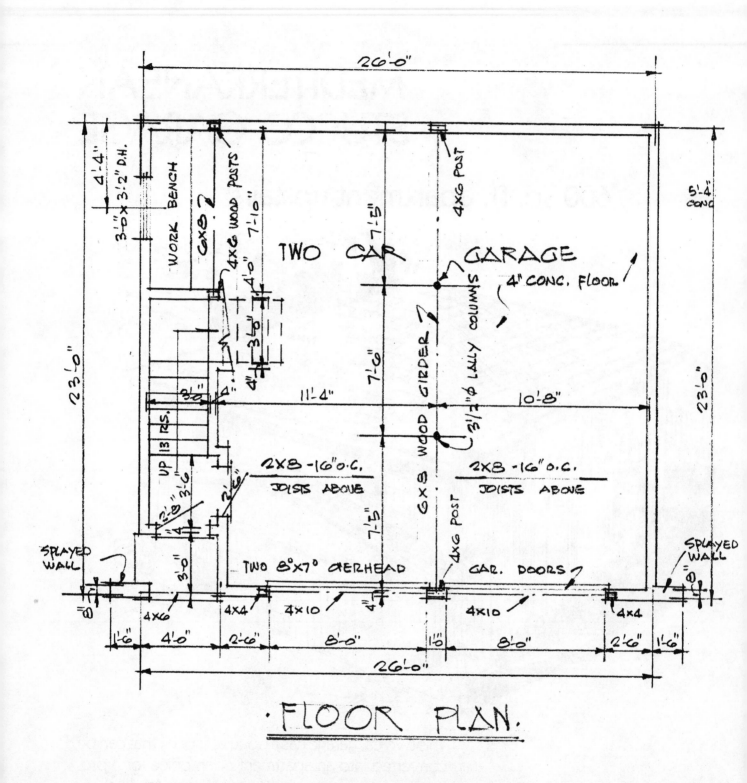

TWO CAR GARAGE

WORK BENCH

4" CONC. FLOOR

4×6 POST

6×8.2

4×6 WOOD POSTS

7'-10"

4'-0"

3'-6"

4"

26'-0"

23'-0"

5'-4" CONC.

23'-0"

7'-5"

7'-6"

7'-5"

3'-0 × 3'-2" D.H.

4'-4"

3" D.

UP 13 RS.

11'-4"

3'-0"

4"

3×8 WOOD GIRDER

3½"∅ LALLY COLUMNS

10'-8"

2×8 -16" O.C.
JOISTS ABOVE

2×8 -16" O.C.
JOISTS ABOVE

4×6 POST

TWO 8°×7° OVERHEAD

CAR. DOORS

SPLAYED WALL

SPLAYED WALL

4×6

4×4

4×10

4"

4×10

4×4

1'-6"

4'-0"

2'-6"

8'-0"

1'-0"

8'-0"

2'-6"

1'-6"

26'-0"

2'-8"

3'-6"

2'-6"

3'-0"

·FLOOR PLAN·

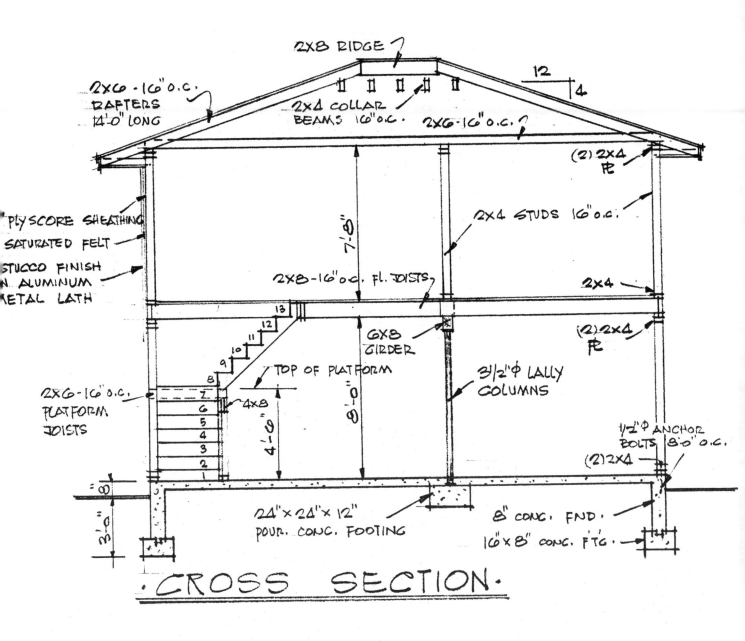

· CROSS SECTION ·

2X8 RIDGE

12 / 4

2X6·16"0.C.
RAFTERS
14'-0" LONG

2X4 COLLAR
BEAMS 16"0.C.

2X6·16"0.C.

(2) 2X4
PL

2X4 STUDS 16"0.C.

PLYSCORE SHEATHING

SATURATED FELT

STUCCO FINISH
ON ALUMINUM
METAL LATH

7'-0"

2X8·16"0.C. FL. JOISTS

2X4

6X8
GIRDER

(2)2X4
PL

TOP OF PLATFORM

3½"∅ LALLY
COLUMNS

2X6·16"0.C.
PLATFORM
JOISTS

4X8

8'-0"

4'-0"

½"∅ ANCHOR
BOLTS 8'-0" O.C.

(2)2X4

24"X 24"X 12"
POUR. CONC. FOOTING

8" CONC. FND.

16"X 8" CONC. FTG·

FRAMING LUMBER LIST			
LOCATION	SIZE	AMOUNT.	LIN. FT.
STUDS	2X4	276/8'	2208
PLATES & SILL	2X4	—	869
RAFTERS	2X6	36/14' 4/16'	568
CEILING JOISTS	2X6	18/12' 18/16'	504
FL. JOISTS	2X8	30/12' 7/16'	472
RIDGE	2X8	—	5

COLLAR BEAMS	2X4	5/10'	50
GIRDER	6X8	1/23' 1/9'	32
DOOR HEADER	4X10	1/18'	18
WOOD POSTS	4X4	4/8'	32
	4X6	3/8'	24

SHEATHING: (□' = SQUARE FEET)
2ND FL. SUB-FLOOR 5/8" PLYWOOD 598□'
SIDE WALLS 3/8" PLYWOOD 1288□'
ROOF ½" PLYWOOD 736□'

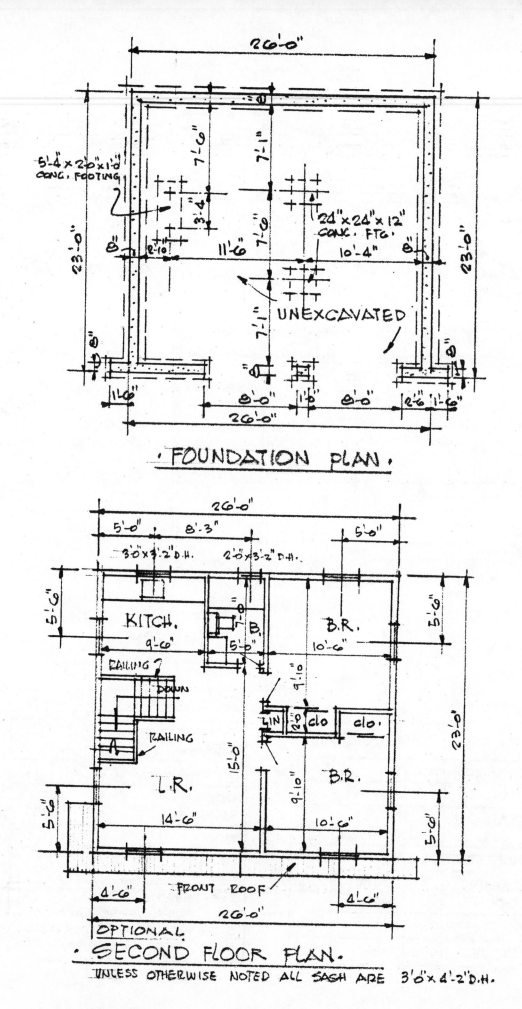

· FOUNDATION PLAN ·

· SECOND FLOOR PLAN ·

UNLESS OTHERWISE NOTED ALL SASH ARE 3'0"x4'-2"D.H.

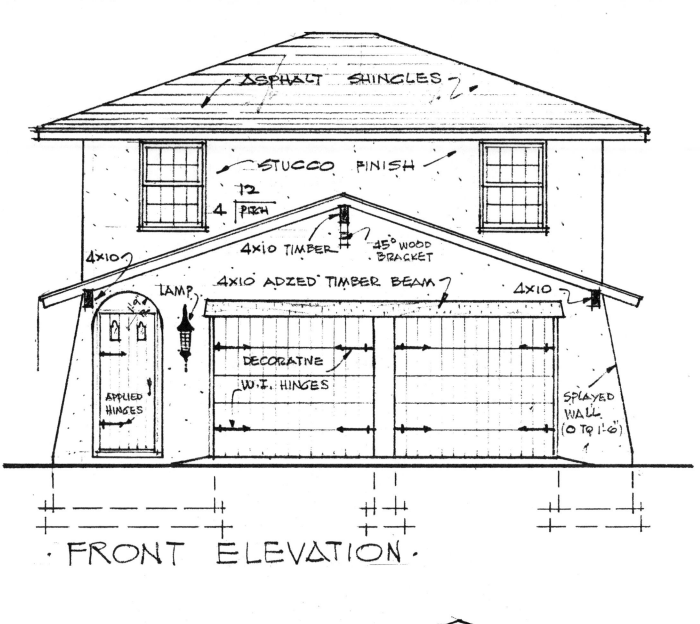

ASPHALT SHINGLES

STUCCO FINISH

12 / 4 PITCH

4×10 TIMBER

45° WOOD BRACKET

4×10 ADZED TIMBER BEAM

4×10

4×10

LAMP

DECORATIVE W.I. HINGES

APPLIED HINGES

SPLAYED WALL (0 TO 1'-6")

· FRONT ELEVATION ·

TWO RAFTERS (2×6s)

FRONT WALL

STUDS

4×10

45° 4×4 BRACKET

2×4

(2) 2×4 ft.

2×8 BOX

4×10

1'6"

4'0"

STUDS

STUDS

FRONT ROOF FRAMING

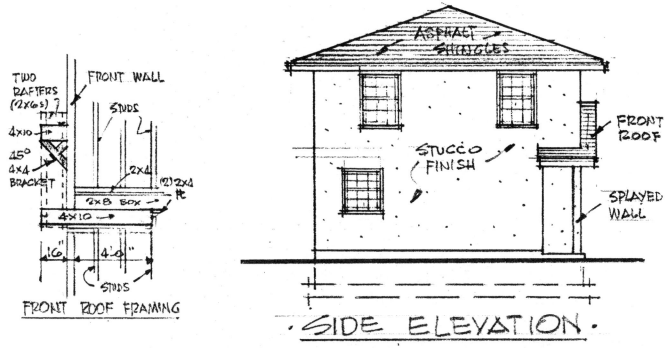

ASPHALT SHINGLES

STUCCO FINISH

FRONT ROOF

SPLAYED WALL

· SIDE ELEVATION ·

23.

Western Barn Garage-Duplex

Also a home where the buffalo roam

This barn garage solves parking problems with two one-car garages. (You can eliminate one if you like.) It also provides a center barn that can be converted into a duplex apartment. On the first floor there is an entry foyer, an 11' x14' room, and a wrap-around stairway. On the second floor there is a full bath and an 11' x14' room. The barn garage is 32' 4" wide, 23' deep for each garage and 26' deep for the center barn. Stain or paint clapboard siding.

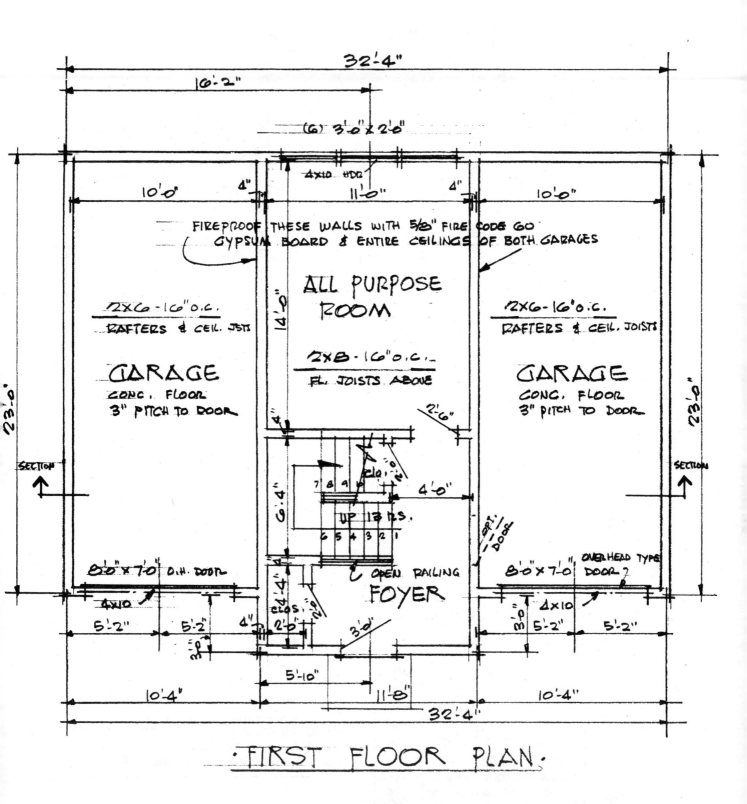

32'-4"

16'-2"

(6) 3'-0" x 2'-0"

4x10 HDR

10'-0"   4"   11'-0"   4"   10'-0"

FIREPROOF THESE WALLS WITH 5/8" FIRE CODE 60
GYPSUM BOARD & ENTIRE CEILINGS OF BOTH GARAGES

ALL PURPOSE
ROOM

12X6 - 16" O.C.
RAFTERS & CEIL. JSTS

12X6 - 16' O.C.
RAFTERS & CEIL. JOISTS

14'-0"

12X8 - 16" O.C.
FL. JOISTS ABOVE

GARAGE
CONC. FLOOR
3" PITCH TO DOOR

GARAGE
CONC. FLOOR
3" PITCH TO DOOR

23'-0"

23'-0"

SECTION

SECTION

2'-6"

9'-4"

CLO.

7 8 9

4'-0"

UP 13 RS.

6 5 4 3 2 1

OPT. DOOR

4'-4"

OPEN RAILING

FOYER

8'-0" X 7'-0" O.H. DOOR

4x10

5'-2"   5'-2"   4"   CLOS.   2'-0"

3'-0"

3'-0"

10'-4"

5'-10"

11'-8"

3'-0"

8'-0" X 7'-0"

OVERHEAD TYPE
DOOR ?

4x10

5'-2"   5'-2"

10'-4"

32'-4"

· FIRST FLOOR PLAN ·

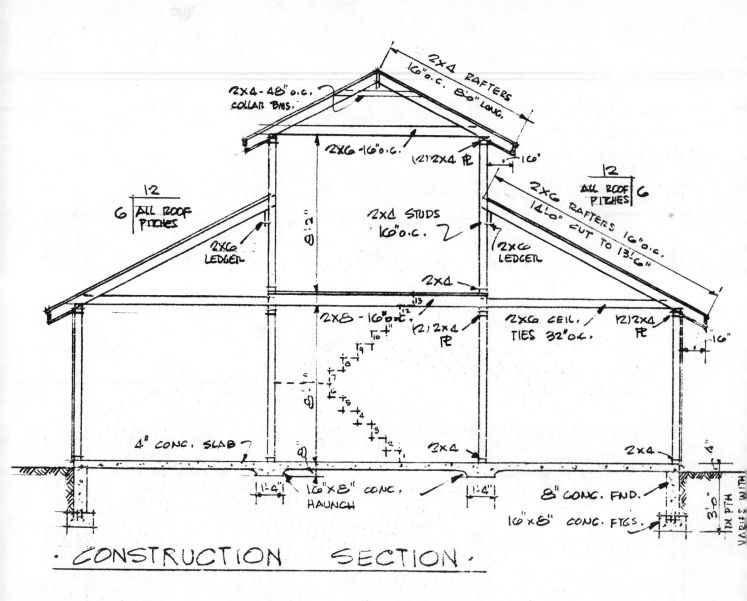

· CONSTRUCTION SECTION ·

FRAMING LUMBER LIST

LOCATION	SIZE	AMT	LIN. FT.
STUDS	2x4	240/8'	1920
PLATES & SILL	2x4	—	614
RAFTERS 2ᴺᴰ FL.	2x4	44/8'	352
CEIL. JOISTS	2x6	20/12' 12/11'	372
FL. JOISTS	2x8	22/12	264
LEDGER	2x6	(2) 23'	46
RIDGE	2x10	1/29'	29
COLLAR BMS.	2x4	6/4'	24
HEADER	2x10	4/10' 4/9'	76
RAFTERS GAR.	2x6	40/14'	560

SQ. FOOTAGE OF SHEATHING AND FINISHING MATERIALS

LOCATION	DESCRIPTION	A···	+10%
SUB-FLOOR	1" PLYWOOD	267.5	293
WALL SHEATHING	½" PLYWOOD	520▫'	572
ROOF SHEATHING	½" PLYWOOD	1195▫'	1314

NOTE: THE WASTE FACTOR IS DETERMINED BY THE TYPE OF MATERIAL USED & THE METHOD OF INSTALLATION.

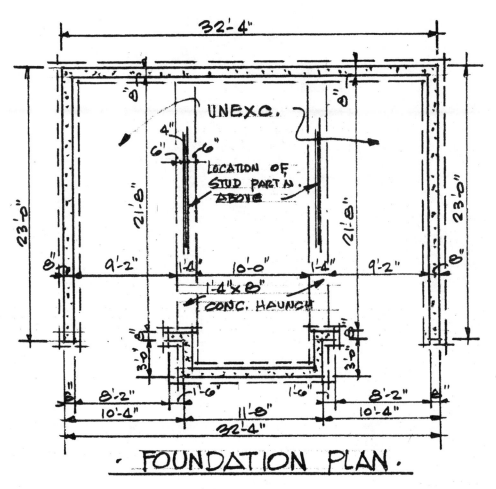

· FOUNDATION PLAN ·

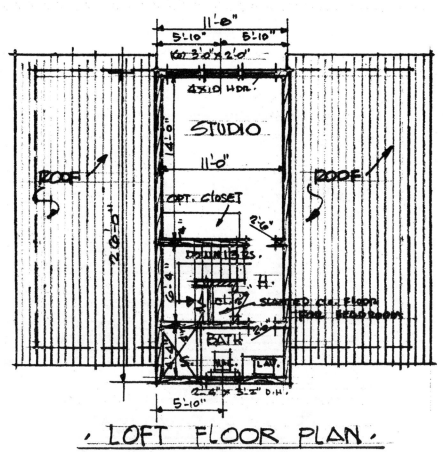

· LOFT FLOOR PLAN ·

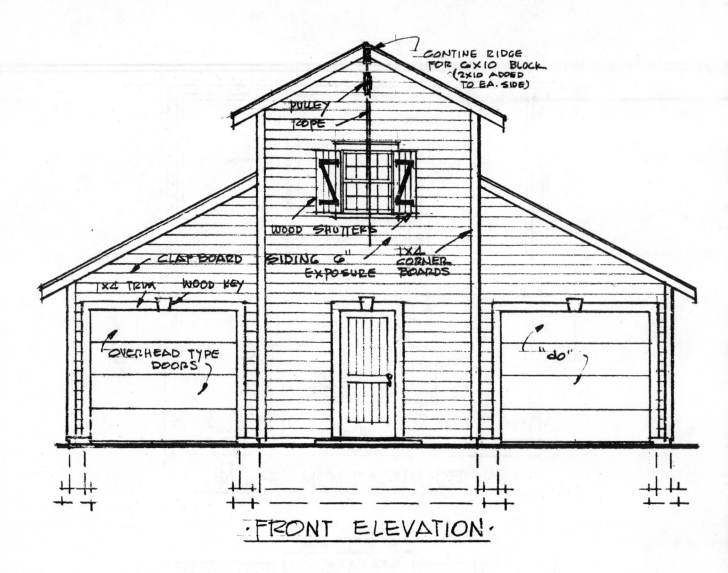

CONTINE RIDGE
FOR 6X10 BLOCK
(2X10 ADDED
TO EA. SIDE)

PULLEY ROPE

WOOD SHUTTERS

CLAPBOARD SIDING 6"
EXPOSURE

1X4 CORNER BOARDS

1X4 TRIM   WOOD KEY

OVERHEAD TYPE DOORS

"do"

·FRONT ELEVATION·

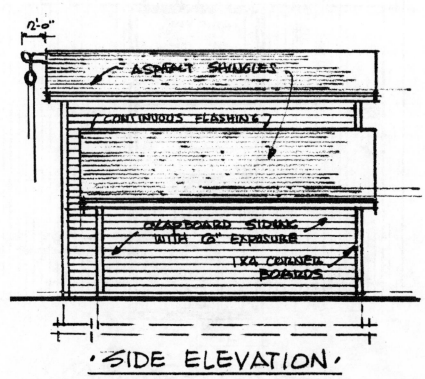

2'-0"

ASPHALT SHINGLES

CONTINUOUS FLASHING

CLAPBOARD SIDING
WITH 6" EXPOSURE

1X4 CORNER BOARDS

· SIDE ELEVATION ·